Basic River Canoeing

By Robert E. McNair

Published by the American Camping Association, Inc.
Bradford Woods
Martinsville, Indiana 46151

Opposite photo courtesy of
Bob Rusher

Third Edition - 1972
Price of $2.95
Standard Book Number 87603-001-0

Library of Congress catalog card number: 70-86467

FOREWORD

This little book is a primer on basic river canoeing. It presents the special skills and knowledge that are so important to those who would travel down our fast flowing rivers in safety.

It was developed for the biannual school of river canoeing that is sanctioned by the Southeastern Pennsylvania Chapter of the American Red Cross and carried out by the canoeing committee of the Buck Ridge Ski Club. This school is known as "Red Ridge College" in canoeing circles. The book and school have been evolving since 1955, following the revolution in techniques that has made white water canoeing safer and more fun than ever.

The goal of "Red Ridge College" is to teach teachers of river canoeing, to teach the new methods to people who would return home to teach others. This more formal edition of the primer should further this same goal on a wider scale. The would-be teachers can learn from it, then distribute copies to those whom they in turn will teach.

This primer does not try to teach all of canoeing. No words have been wasted teaching what the readily available Red Cross and Boy Scout books teach so well. The common lore is assumed to be well known to the student so full concentration may be put on the new techniques that have revolutionized river canoeing and yet are little known outside the white water clubs. There is likewise no intent to teach advanced wild water canoeing. One chapter discusses it, but the objective here is to teach fundamentals of safe river canoeing for the masses who would coast down our rivers in ordinary commercially available open canoes.

Many have helped. They wrote parts of earlier versions, drew sketches, corrected revisions, and wrestled with the problems of printing. Very special thanks go to Jim Calkins, Mark Fawcett, Edith McNair, Fletcher MacNeill, Bobbie and Don Rupp, Bob Rusher, Lloyd Vye, and Jeff Wilhoyte. John Fitch, friend to "Red Ridge College," brought final success by printing the first edition.

Bob McNair
Swarthmore, Pa.
January, 1969

CONTENTS

INTRODUCTION

Though you intend to become a teacher, you probably must first lear modern river canoeing. Older books imply that you learn through years c experience, but this is no longer so. Today you are taught refined skill: and clever strategems for specific recognizable and recurrent situations You can never improvise by yourself what so many have spent the past tei years developing.

You may learn these skills and strategems from this book or from a weekend course, but do not think you are then a skilled white water canoe- ist. A talking acquaintance is not enough. You must practice the approved strokes and the special tactics. You must train your eye to read the water. You must develop judgment through experience. For this practice you must paddle with a group.

Find a white water club. Even if they do not give formal instruction you will be safer and learn more among canoeists who are more expert than you. As you follow the lead, observe his decisions and learn to under- stand them. You will make some mistakes and appreciate the rescue skills.

Some readers will not find experienced clubs in their area. Perhaps you are in a group where all will be learning together. If you are a loner you will just have to gather a group that can learn together. As teacher you will be only a little ahead of your students. You must emphasize per- fecting skills in safe situations before you apply them where they are really needed. Encourage "playing the river." Convince your friends that they are out for fun and that fun is not measured in miles traveled but in hours spent in rapids. Do not rush through rapids but stay and play at forward ferries and eddy turns before going on to look for the next fun spot. When you really need the skills they will have been practiced and perfected.

Read the other canoeing books also and have your people read them. You will not be able to explain everything to everybody while canoeing. A different point of view will sometimes help you but be very wary of old notions and misstatements.

Your canoeing education will be furthered by visiting a slalom. Look at the equipment, talk to the people, and study the paddlers. It is best of all to enter. You will learn skills that serve you well in wilderness rapids. Your group will learn much by setting a small slalom just for practice. The slalom gates compel a very exact course without any boat smashing penalties on those who fail.

Always keep learning. The sport is still developing rapidly and you will be left behind if you stop learning. Paddle with other clubs. Be humble and receptive so you can learn any little thing that they may know and you don't. Be receptive to new ideas but don't be swept off your feet. You will see things that are out of date or downright wrong. What you learn today may be wrong tomorrow. Just keep learning, keep an open mind, keep thinking.

Now that you have the overall learning process in mind let us get on with this primer. For good learning purposes we artificially divide river canoeing into chapters on equipment, paddle strokes, water reading, maneuvering tactics, rescue, and overall strategy.

EQUIPMENT AND CLOTHING

Canoes, like canoeing skills, have been highly perfected over the past century. Despite their rich history, however, they are still evolving. Any canoe design is a compromise: maneuverability against speed, strength against lightness, and so on. Here we will discuss only the new mix of old concepts that is needed for the white water canoe. Unfortunately few of today's canoes were designed for white water so we must accept unwanted compromises with flat water speed, economics, and convention.

The traditional canoe is the canvas covered wooden canoe. A thing of beauty is a joy forever. Their lines make these canoes a delight on quiet water. A few had lines for fast water, but this use is obsolete now that stronger materials are available. Old wood canoes become heavy with repeated varnishing, weak and heavy with repeated wetting. The bottoms may go round with age and spoil both stability and maneuverability. The skillful and cautious paddler can bring these wood canoes through safely but it takes too many canoes to become skillful. The economics are against them but hopefully esthetics will guard their future for quiet water. The cedar canoe, all wood and no canvas, is swifter, less maneuverable, more fragile, and more beautiful.

Fiber glass canoes have great promise. Here is strength and also the flexibility to give rather than break when hit against rocks. There is no upkeep, and no increase in weight from being painted or soaking up water. Fiber glass slides over rock more easily than aluminum. It repairs well. Molds are cheaper than the dies for forming aluminum canoes so that special shapes for the limited white water market are economic. Unfortunately there are only a few white water models in very limited production - except in Europe where absence of aluminum canoes gave greater urgency to fiber glass for white water. In America the major companies selling fiber glass canoes design them for flat water. They have large keels on the outside. Most have round bottoms so they will paddle straight on flat water but they lack maneuverability for fast water. Their flotation is adequate for still water, but safety in white water upsets requires much more flotation. It should be placed to make the on-end dumping method effective.

Today the special fiber glass canoe for slalom and white water is rapidly attaining perfection. It is completely decked over with cockpits fore and aft. The paddlers wear spray skirts to seal the openings. Inside are knee straps and foot braces, a thwart to lean against. A flattish rocker bottom gives them maneuverability, and an elliptical cross section and narrow beam make them eskimo rollable. Both the one and two-man versions are superb boats. They are not intended for touring. Duffel capacity is limited and the single low kneeling position becomes cramped after long hours afloat. The fiber glass slalom canoe is the sportster of canoeing.

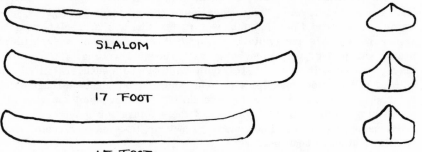

SLALOM

17 FOOT

15 FOOT

Aluminum is still preeminent for white water cruising canoes. Aluminum canoes are tougher than fiber glass for the same weight (a tough alloy must be used). They come in shapes that are good compromises between speed and maneuverability. However, we do not recommend all aluminum canoes. We have seen some with round bottoms, or soft aluminum, or with inadequate flotation. The leading make is very good and there is merit in standardization in a canoe fleet. The fifteen and seventeen foot models are most popular. The fifteen is very maneuverable and good for day trips. With a splash cover it is good in heavy water. However, when loaded it pushes a bow wave so the sleeker seventeen is to be preferred for extended trips. In either case buy standard weight (not light weight) for white water and do pay extra for the shoe keel. The shoe keel is a must for white water.

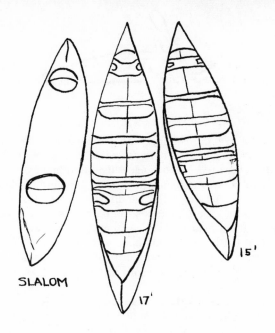

SLALOM   17'   15'

The white water canoe of the future is difficult to foresee. Perhaps it will be a blunt nosed, rocker bottomed, banana shaped boat in aluminum. Perhaps it will have much more flotation, cleverly placed so that after an upset even a beginner can brace his feet, pull on a strap, and bring the canoe upright, empty of water. However dramatic the improvements of the past ten years, there are more yet to come.

Kayaks and foldboats are beyond our scope but a comment is in order. For the beginner they are easier to handle in quiet water, but white water handling is a fine skill little known outside white water circles. The fiber glass single is tops. The foldboat is to be avoided unless you must carry it in an elevator. Doubles are not for white water, and neither are the stick and canvas kayaks that kids build. If someone joshes you about paddling an old fashioned canoe tell them your canoe is sociable, costs less per person is adapted to breaking in neophytes, carries more provisions, portages more easily, and allows more paddling positions for comfort after long hours afloat. Tell them you can go anywhere they can too. There should be some kayaks in your club. They are sporting.

Canoe seats are interestingly controversial. The Indians didn't use them and why should we. The Red Cross and the Scouts agree that t h e seats should be omitted. The Buck Ridge aluminum fleet has seats. We wouldn't think of removing them. They add strength of course. They al - so provide for a variety of relief paddling positions for long hours afloat. Extended periods of kneeling makes the legs so stiff you could not possibly scramble over the rocks to help someone. It is better to sit in qui e t stretches, PROVIDED your knees have a firm hold on the gunwales. T h e leader must crack down on any who fail to kneel in rapids. Let us disci - pline our paddlers and leave the seats in.

It sometimes happens that a man has trouble extricating his big feet from under a low bow seat after a spill. F o·r t h i s reason a few people remove the bow seat in white water season and replace it wit h a simple thwart or with a homemade seat at gunwale height.

Center thwarts should be almost exactly at the center of gravity. We load, unload, and portage our canoes many times oftener than we so lo paddle them. Drill an extra set of holes and use wing nuts if you want to solo paddle, but keep the thwart set for solo portaging.

Knee straps are very important. They give a firm hold on the canoe and complete control while your hands are properly busy with the paddle. You will have fewer spills and when you do spill you fall free of the straps. Once you have tried them you will be amazed at the confidence they give you and you will never want to enter a rapid again without them.

To install straps in your aluminum canoe you must first rivet the anchor strips to the floor. Cut strips 1 inch wide by 6 inches long from a sheet of hardened aluminum such as is supplied for patching canoes. Bend them up in the center to allow a strap about 1-1/2 inches wide to pass under. Drill two rivet holes in each end. Two are needed for each end of the canoe. Rivet them in so the strap anchors come 3 inches to the right and left of the keel and about 4 inches back of the front of your knee when you kneel. A single strap about 8 feet long with a good strong buckle is strung as shown below. At the top and rear the strap passes around the seat thwart. It is also common to see canoes with a single ring on the keel and taut straps right to the gunwale above. Such straps may need toe blocks to keep you forward so they are tight on your thighs.

Knee pads are popular. There must be two because your knees are spread wide apart in the bilges. Most people buy the strap on type that hardware stores supply for gardeners and roofers. Some would rather glue pads in the canoe to avoid any catching on knee straps after spills. Sponge rubber of the closed cell type is good but still sops up water. A very cheap type (since they do get lost) is a segment of inner tube with sawdust sealed in.

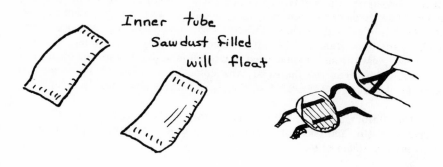

Inner tube
Sawdust filled
will float

Painters for white water canoes should be 3/8 inch in diameter and 10 to 15 feet in length. This large width is not for strength, but so a man can pull harder without cutting his hands. Seize the ends to prevent unlaying. Do not use monkey firsts or floats since they get wedged between rocks. Put painters at bow and stern, and fasten at the extreme ends within a few inches of the water line. It is important that painters not be knotted or wrapped around thwarts because they must be free to stream out in an upset.

Splash covers become more numerous each year. There are those who say that splash covers take away the challenge of picking your way through waves. I would not neglect developing this skill in the complete canoeist, but there are arguments the other way too. You may run much heavier water than before and you can put heart and soul into mastering the canoe and the waves instead of cringing, fearing to do anything drastic for fear of shipping water. The advantage of splash covers in ice water canoeing is obvious. One of the greatest hazards to canoe teams is the multiple upset which usually occurs at flood water. Even an unsplash covered fleet wants a few splash covered rescue boats at this moment. It is interesting to note that smaller canoes can be used when they are covered. Thus the fifteen footer, which is lighter and more maneuverable, comes into its own for rugged water. (The longer canoes wrap around rocks more easily.)

Obtaining a splash cover is difficult. A day will come when they may be bought and when canoes will be designed for them. Today you must make your own. Most are of rubberized nylon, held on with a row of snaps below the gunwale. Even when the material is preshrunk, these sometimes shrink so the snaps do not reach. Put fasteners, not snaps, at the bow so wave plunging will not pull it off. On important runs put adhesive tape around to stop seepage. Some people try a low ridge pole so it cannot hold a deckload of water. We have seen covers of plywood, aluminum, and fiber glass. The latter seems best. The fiber glass is bent over the gunwale and an ashwood strip holds it tight with sheet metal screws. Whatever the material, the cockpit holes should be standard size (oval, about 17" x 19") so that spray skirts are interchangeable.

The slalom canoe which is permanently decked and needs only spray skirts is better and cheaper. However, it is nice to have a splash cover for your aluminum also.

Paddles for white water should be of hard wood or fiber glass with aluminum shaft. Ash is very good. Maple is strong but heavy; it will split unless you strip the varnish off your new paddle and soak the blade in linseed oil. The trend is to shorter paddles, about to your chin for aluminum canoes (and a few inches shorter yet for slalom canoes with their lower kneeling position and narrower hulls). Blades should be seven to eight inches in width. Narrower wastes energy, wider is clumsy. The grip should be rather square or T-shaped (not rounded) so you can feel the exact angle of your blade. These paddle specifications are not rigid but depend on your physique and your preference.

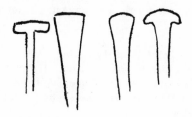

Life jackets must in some states be types that are approved by the Coast Guard. However, their criteria are not those of white water canoeing. Some that meet with their approval are inadequate; some of the best for white water are not approved. Get the best for your safety.

For rapids you need lots of flotation. You need both flotation and padding on your back (when you float on your back in frothy water the flotation on your chest is useless). It should be streamlined for swimming and low drag, it should give freedom to paddle, and you should be able to climb into your canoe while wearing it. The ideal life jacket has not yet been invented.

See what your friends are wearing and look around. There are some good looking foreign ones turning up at slaloms. The cellular pneumatic ones that won't sink after a single puncture seem promising. Whatever you get, test it swimming rapids, climbing into the canoe from the water, perhaps even eskimo rolling.

Clothing for canoeing ranges from bathing suits to mittens. It is dic-tated by comfort, safety, and durability rather than by fashion. It must keep you warm, or cool, or perhaps dry, and it must withstand water and mud, and hard wear.

Woolen long johns head the list for safety. They should be worn from October to May when the water is cold. The wool right next to your skin keeps you warm even when wet. It is a matter of comfort when your legs are wet all day long and it is a matter of survival when you spill into cold water. Buy fancy ones at ski shops or tough scratchy ones at an army surplus store.

Wet suits are a must for rough rivers in early spring. When eskimo rolling is the order of the day, long johns just won't do. Unfortunately, wet suits are expensive. They also tear easily, bunch up behind your knee, and get overly warm. Perhaps they inspired the saying, "Old river rats never die. They just smell that way."

Shoes are a must in white water. Otherwise an unexpected jump-out may cut your feet on sharp rocks or the ever present glass. In summer use sneakers with lots of holes to let the water out. (The holes appear by themselves.) Moccasins are too easily lost. In cooler weather you will want wool socks. In early spring wet sneakers are miserable wool socks or no. An older solution was the light leather and rubber shoepack. But today it is better to wear wet suit socks inside oversize sneakers. They are warmer, less likely to catch in knee straps, and better for swimming.

Foul weather gear can be a blessing, but make it light. Raincoats dribble through in front and ponchos are good only when you want to be blown downwind. Rain suits are good.

In general it is better to have many light layers of clothes. Some prefer close fitting sweaters to loose shirts for better temperature control. A windbreaker is very good, but avoid a long heavy jacket. Trousers, rather than shorts, may be worn even in summer to protect the knees from sun, gnats, brambles, and kneeling. A cap can keep sunglare from your eyes, sun off your nose, or water off your glasses. Sunglasses, particularly polaroids, are worthwhile when running rapids into the sun. Use your own ingenuity from here. Someday you will wish you had thought o f mittens and will find that you can paddle with wool socks on your hands.

A change of dry clothes may be placed in your pick up car or carried with you in waterproof bags.

Those black, rectangular rubber bags with roll down, fold in, buckle down tops are really waterproof and can be found in army surplus stores. They come in three sizes: lunch and camera, spare clothes and sleeping bag size.

The khaki rubber sacks are hard to tie tightly and they easily spring leaks from abrasion. Still they are useful inside conventional knapsacks.

Remember a few large packs are best, not a lot of little bundles stuck and tied all over your canoe. Be sure EVERYTHING is tied in, but don't lash it: wet knots cause difficulty in salvage operations. Straps and snap rings are good enough so packs will not dangle out after upsets.

Eye glasses must be tied on too. Buy clips or use any old string. The ear pieces of plastic frames are often drilled for string. Some contact lenses are lost in spills.

Camera boxes can be made out of the toggle clamp ammunition boxes. It is quicker to get your camera out (and to stow it again) than when you use those black rubber bags. You may want to bolt the box right into your canoe and you will certainly want to test that the gasket holds water out. Special waterproof camera bags are available from Klepper.

What not to take is also important. You do better to leave your wallet and watch behind or put them in the bottom of your bag. Diamond rings are likely to come off when the hands are cold and wet. A friend plans his canoe camping by putting his gear in three piles: the essentials, the almost essentials, and the luxuries. He takes all of the first pile, none of the second, and a single item from the third. A check list, as on the next page, keeps you from forgetting essentials. It is only a reminder and you do not take all the things listed. There is luxury in going light.

EQUIPMENT CHECK LIST

Take only things you will need.

EQUIPMENT

CANOE, Knee Straps, Bow and Stern Painters
3 Paddles and Twine
Life Preservers, Knee Pads, Helmets
Splash Cover, Spray Skirts
Bailing Scoop (from Clorox bottle), Sponge
Canoe Patch Kit
Small Waterproof Bag
Camera and Film
Topo Maps, Compass, Jacknife
First Aid Kit
Lunch, Canteen
2 Sets of Car Keys

CLOTHING

Woolen Long Johns
Warm Trousers or Slacks, Woolen Sweaters
Cotton Shirts, Wind Breaker, Cap, Mittens
Spare Set of Dry Clothes
Rain Gear
Sneakers, Wool Socks
Wet Suit, Wet Suit Socks (inside sneakers)
Swim Suit
Sun Glasses, String for Glasses, Sun Tan Lotion
Towel, Yellow Soap (for poison ivy)
Money, Lunch

OVERNIGHT

Sleeping Bag and/or Blankets
Tent (with mosquito netting), Ground Cloth
Air Mattress
Cook Kit, Matches, Candle
Food
Stove
Hatchet, Ax, or Saw
Flashlight
Large Waterproof Pack, Ditty Bag
Extra Rope
Toilet Kit, Fly Dope
Fishing Tackle

MAKING YOUR PADDLE STROKES MORE EFFECTIVE

This is a discussion of river paddling technique. We assume the reader is already familiar with the Red Cross canoeing book and its descriptions of paddle strokes. Every stroke is useful at some time for the varied demands of the river canoeist. All the strokes should be mastered. However, when we run rivers we must by habit perform each tactic in the one best way. Automatically and without hesitation our paddle must fly into action with the one best stroke for that situation, even though our conscious thought be preoccupied with whether there is a rock under that wave, or whether we can reach the safety of the eddy beyond. Not only is there no time to check that your draw is really perpendicular, but there is no time to think whether you should use a draw. All that must be automatic. Habit must produce the one best way, not some alternative way of accomplishing the same end. So here we shall concentrate on those strokes that you must fall back on when the chips are down.

It is always a problem to learn how to make our strokes more effective. Partly we must make our decision faster to allow more time for action. Partly the paddle must move quickly to take more strokes in the time of grace. Then the technique must be perfected in sympathy with your physique so that you get the maximum effectiveness from your strength. In this light let us discuss the key river strokes.

THE BACK STROKE

The back stroke comes first. This is because it is first in importance in a crisis. It is the stroke for back ferrying to safety; it is the stroke to give you more time to think when you can go neither right nor left and the prospect ahead is disturbing. It is the stroke to ease the blow when all else has failed. We even teach this stroke first on occasion because we note a tendency to revert to the most familiar stroke when flustered. All too often this is the forward stroke and drives the canoe toward catastrophe. It is important that the back stroke be practiced for long distances in still water so that you feel at home doing it and so that you know how to put your strength into it. It is difficult for the stern man to hold course when moving backward, just as it is hard for the bow man to steer by himself when moving forward. The bow man must learn to put small reverse J's on his back stroke to help in holding a true course.

There is a variation on this stroke which some people favor. If you turn the hand at the top of the paddle around so your palm pushes the paddle grip back toward your face, it is said to bring different and more powerful muscles into play. This could be important in river canoeing. Some paddlers find this hand position facilitates blending from draw to back stroke on a back ferry toward the stern man's paddling side. Others think the hand shift just wastes time.

BACK

FORWARD

THE DRAW

The draw stroke is second only to the back stroke in importance. It is well known but some aspects should be emphasized for river people who must put great reliance on the draw.

When you draw, your canoe moves sideways only because you have pulled water in the opposite direction and propelled the water under the canoe. What splashes against the canoe not only wets the paddler, but also reduces the power of the stroke. Keep your paddle deep.

A diagonal draw pulls the canoe forward as well as sideways. When you are trying to miss a rock you do not want to pull forward, yet many paddlers do just that when flustered. Learn a pure draw with the paddle directly out from your shoulder and no forward component whatever. Some paddlers twist their body to face their draw stroke, but you must still look where you are going.

The blending of draw and forward stroke into the diagonal draw is convenient for mild situations after your basic habit has been formed.

The draw is most effective if you can keep the power on right up to the canoe and use a very quick recovery. Beginners often catch the paddle on the canoe or sluff off at the end of the stroke. A fast, clean retrieval can be effected by putting the top of the paddle forward and in front of you, with a quick twist of the shaft so the blade slices out of the water on the aft diagonal. This instant recovery will improve your drawing power.

Advanced paddlers should realize that the draw stroke has a righting effect on the canoe. This is contrary to the layman's expectation that the draw would tip you over toward the paddling side. The reason is that the water force on the paddle is well below the surface while the water drag on the canoe is right at the surface. If the knees are properly holding the canoe, you will see that the canoe does indeed tip away from the paddling side as soon as the power is applied. This is important because it allows you to lean far out without falling in or tipping over while you are pulling on the paddle and so allows longer, more powerful draws. This bracing force stops when you stop pulling, so you had better retrieve fast or stop leaning at the end of the stroke.

THE PRYAWAY

The pushaway is the best known opposite to the draw stroke. For white water the pushaway is lacking in power. A more powerful version of the same stroke has been developed and this is called the "pryaway." There is controversy over whether to teach this stroke before or after the cross draw. It is a difficult stroke for beginners and can tip over the beginner's canoe. Yet, if cross draw becomes the habitual opposite to draw, it will capsize canoes in heavy water. We teach pryaway first. At least it is just an extension of the pushaway learned in Boy Scouts or Red Cross.

For this stroke we use a feathered underwater recovery because it is faster and less awkward than aerial recovery. (The aerial recovery is still the preferred way for draw strokes.) If beginners will learn their pushaway with this underwater recovery, It will ease their later conver- tion to the pryaway.

There is more power in actually prying the paddle off the bilge of the canoe. Don't bother pushing the paddle away from the canoe. When the paddle is a little beyond vertical, go back under for another pry.

Now the stroke must be made longer. Slide the paddle down deeper in the water, letting your bottom hand slide up six inches from the throat. Then start the stroke further under the canoe; the top of the paddle must be beyond the gunwale, actually over the water at the start. This stroke is done beside your knee and not directly out from the shoulder as is the draw. Beginners may need the steadying effect of the bottom hand near the gunwale (but not holding it). However, it is better to have both hands above the gunwale so both arms can pull. Then the weight of the shoulders can be thrown against the pull of the paddle.

This then is the pryaway of the river man, the stroke that must be used in heavy water. If it feels awkward and insecure, then you must practice it more until it beomes just as powerful as your draw.

THE CROSS DRAW

We learned the cross draw from the Appalachian Mountain Club some fifteen years ago and found it a wonderful stroke for dodging through shallow rock gardens. It was easily learned by beginners along with its counterpart, the draw, in the very first lesson. When we ventured into more difficult water, we found serious disadvantages. The paddle spends too much time flying over the bow in going from side to side. It is an isolated stroke and can not be blended into the strokes that went before and will come after. Its most serious shortcoming is that it has no bracing action. The paddle blade pulls at the surface, not a half blade down, and there is no righting force. Today we tell you to throw your body into your strokes. Don't throw yourself into a cross draw: stay right over the canoe and just reach with the arms. Many spills in slalom and heavy water result from unexpected cross draws. The stern man can brace, but he is neglecting other duties in compensating for a cross draw.

However, the cross draw is a nice stroke in its place and here is how it goes. The paddle is swung over the bow to the offside somewhat as in the cross bow rudder, but you don't just brace it, you swing it. The draw throws the water under the canoe. The cross draw throws the water in front of the bow,  or just under it. Be sure the top of the paddle is down within a few inches of the gunwale so the paddle is almost parallel with the water. Swing your shoulders. A forward lean helps you throw the water in front of your bow.

It is a nice stroke for beginners, an easy way to go from right to left without committing that dreadful sin of switching hands. It is also nice for delicate bow women. The blade is well forward and has a better turning moment. On a side slip the bow man moves only the bow and leaves two thirds of the canoe for his muscular stern man. It is effective in shallow water because the blade is horizontal and draws little water even when the whole blade is pulling. Still, the cross draw must not become the habitual counterpart of the draw. Teach it second. Use it only intermittently.

THE REVERSE QUARTER SWEEP

The reverse quarter sweep is often used in river canoeing to set the angle for a back ferry. This sometimes takes great power and this is achieved by starting the b l a d e way under the stern and prying all around the canoe hull. It is a sort of pryaway displaced to the rear.

Some paddlers use the conventional reverse quarter sweep without pry, but this is mainly in slalom boats. You should e x p e r iment to find the most effective way for you in your canoe.

THE J STROKE

The J stroke is important to white water canoeing even though most river maneuvering is not the steering of lake paddling. A forward stroke is needed that can give a quick correction or drastic oversteering without slowing or breaking a sprint paddling tempo.

In perfecting the conventional J stroke, be sure first that the thumb of the top hand turns down and that the paddle is given a small power hook and not just trailed as a rudder. A common fault is that the thumb does not turn down far enough. It must turn the paddle shaft ninety degrees or the hook is ineffective. Another common fault of inexperienced paddlers is that the paddle is across their chest and not vertical as illustrated below.

Like This   Not This

The pitch stroke version should be known to the complete canoeist even though the hook J is best for beginners and white water. In the pitch version the paddle is angled half way through the stroke and pulled the rest of the way at this angle. There is no hook at the end. The steering force comes from forcing the paddle to continue in a straight line though held at an angle. This is a restful variation for flat water paddling. It does not give the overcorrections needed for white water.

A third variation is sometimes used for slalom canoes in white water. Here the thumb is turned up instantly and the paddle is given a quick pry off the boat for the correction.

The C stroke, the version used in single canoeing, is just as essential in white water canoeing as in flat water canoeing. The technique is the same as described in the Red Cross and Scout books so it will not be described here.

THE BOW OR FORWARD STROKE

The forward stroke comes almost naturally and should not be stressed until the back stroke, draw, and pryaway are well in mind. Then careful attention should be given to the forward stroke. Even if you have no racing aspirations, you want to paddle all day without tiring. A common inefficiency is lifting the paddle on the recovery. If you will swing it in a wide arc, feathered and close to the water, then the bottom arm remains relaxed with no lifting to be done. It is usual to teach that the bottom arm should relax and not pull, that the drive goes into the top of the paddle from the top arm, the shoulders, and the back. It is probably good to paddle with both arms straight while learning to put your back muscles to work. The power part of the stroke is short. It comes where the paddle is near ly vertical. In racing the stroke may be short and choppy with a high tempo, while in cruising a coasting entry and a relaxed get ready to recover makes the stroke look longer than it really is. The paddle should be close to vertical as viewed from behind. This is an important point to watch for when coaching back stroke, J stroke, or forward stroke. One reason is that the canoe goes straighter with the blade running closer to the keel line. The important point is that if the blade is out to the side there is a twisting moment not suited to our bodies, while with the paddle under-neath we can pour the power in with our body driving straight forward, or back. Note that slalom kayakers also use a vertical stroke nowadays.

We really have much to learn about better forward strokes. You will be on the right track if you will relax right up to the big push, and then put your whole body strength into that paddle.

THE SCULLING STROKE

Sculling is sometimes useful because it gives a continuous stroke without a recovery hiatus. The sculling draw may be useful when rocks are too close for a normal draw. Sculling is sometimes mixed with a low brace or a high brace for a more prolonged effect.

THE LOW BRACE

The paddle brace is the great contribution of kayaking to canoeing and the most significant addition to canoeing skills in many years. At last we put full reliance in our paddle and use it not only to propel the canoe in any direction, but also to steady it, to lean it into turns, to correct impending capsize, and even to right the canoe from an upside down position. There are different varieties of braces and we start with the low brace.

Here the paddle is laid flat on the water, the palm of the top hand is up, and the wrist of the throat hand is high. If you are capsizing to that side a quick down push will right you. You do not slap the water but the down thrust is lightning fast and powerful. In an extreme crisis you will throw your body and head down into the water bringing the canoe around with your knees and hips, and will only bring your body back aboard at the very end, just as in an eskimo roll. In treacherous spots we sometimes run in a "ready brace" position. That is, the paddle is in position but no push - unless. Perhaps the most common use of the low brace is in an eddy turn or a peel off when it is the stern man's brace. Here there is the added duty of holding the canoe on its side to present the bottom to the onrushing water. This means hanging out so the body weight pulls the canoe over. Sometimes you want to carry part of your weight on the blade so you can lean even further. It should be noted that the canoe could flip in either direction. One way is corrected with the downthrust which is the brace proper. The other is corrected by your full weight hanging so far to the side.

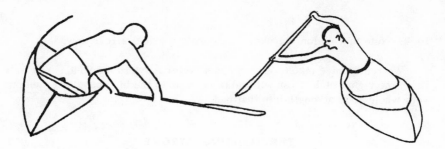

Low Brace   High Brace

THE HIGH BRACE

In some places you need a brace, a draw, and a canoe lean all at once. This is particularly true when it is the bow man's brace and draw on entering an eddy or peeling off.   The top arm is now straight to hold the top of the paddle high. This gives it drawing action. The extreme lean and reach bank the canoe, the bracing action comes either from the angle off vertical or from the depth of the blade. Too much angle will spoil the canoe lean, so hold the top hand high and bury the blade deep. If you sud - denly need a righting moment, just pull harder or go into a low brace. With a sharp eddy and a responsive canoe a single lean, grab, draw will bring the canoe around and up into the eddy.

RUNNING POSITION

When your captain shouts "O.K." he means do nothing, as opposed to forward, back, left, or right. It is important that you know how to do "nothing" well! Today we coast with our paddle vertical in the water about a foot from the canoe, ready to go in any direction. Holding the paddle across your chest is obsolete because it takes too long to initiate action. However, in severe wave plunging some compromise position may be better and in treacherous spots the low brace position may better anticipate the next problem.

DON'T SHIFT SIDES

The Red Cross and the Boy Scouts correctly teach that the stern man shall paddle on one side, the bow man on the other, and that they shall not shift sides indiscriminately. In the evolution of river canoeing, however, there was a period in which the paddler flipped his paddle back and forth so he could use his most effective stroke. When we study movies of such paddlers, we are surprised at the indecision and at the time the paddle spends waving uselessly in the air. It would appear that such paddlers have not disciplined themselves to learn the strokes that give any desired effect from a single side. In modern heavy water canoeing you must know that your partner will stick to his side, ready to throw a brace if the need arises. In doubles canoeing there is no preferred side. The pryaway is just as effective as the draw. The backhand grip for the back stroke makes it easy to blend between draw and back stroke and makes back ferries equally effective from either side. For solo canoeing there is still an argument, but for C-2 the temporary need of the evolving sport is past. Don't change sides!

IN CONCLUSION

All the other strokes will be used sooner or later, but it is best that a minimum number of basic strokes be learned to perfection first and used while learning water reading and tactics, and so become the paddler's habitual and automatic strokes. Do not confuse the student with the lesser strokes at this time. Later they will find that the bow sweep has a place in slalom boat pivots, that the bow rudder can be modified into the slice, pry, drive of eddy turns, while the sculling pushaway is generally useless.

A stroke is learned when you get the most out of it for the strength which you can put in. Most people feel that full strength should not be put into a stroke until the form is perfect. True, but you will never know whether your form is perfect until you can put in full strength and still be smooth. Many paddlers have never discovered the power at their command when it is really needed. Nevertheless, making a quick, correct decision and using the most effective stroke performed in the most efficient manner are what will make you the better paddler.

The wonderfully effective new techniques of handling the paddle have general attributes which you should understand.

Since you have knee straps, your legs take care of the canoe and your hands are devoted entirely to the paddle. Watch for students who clutch at gunwales, grab for branches, or push off rocks. Tell them to put their faith in their paddle and their paddle in the water. The new strokes are magic.

Note how many of the strokes require precision angle control from the hand on top of the paddle, not only the J, but the pryaway, the draw, and bracing.

Finally note how the whole body becomes involved. The legs control the canoe, stomach muscles transmit the draw power to the boat, back muscles drive you forward. Throw your shoulder weight into the pryaway and back stroke, lean into the draws and braces. Learn to use your entire body. The agile and well coordinated paddler of today outperforms the musclebound husky of yesterday.

CHAPTER 4
THE ART OF READING FAST WATER.

There is beauty in fast water. The patterns and colors are a painting and the sounds are a symphony. These matters you must discover for yourself. I am going to discuss some prosaic aspects of river rapids. They will help you to see rocks where none are visible and to see clear passages where only chaos greets the untutored eye.

The first factor to consider with moving water is its tremendous power. Coasting through a river rapid at ten miles an hour may seem tame, but you are deceived. Before you conduct any expensive tests, let me analyze a situation. Suppose your canoe is pinned on a rock perpendicular to the current. The force of the water on the canoe is the area the canoe presents to the water times the water velocity squared times 2.8. (This presumes a drag coefficient of 1.) Since the current is ten miles an hour the force on your fifteen foot canoe is about $15 \times 2 \times 10^2 \times 2.8 = 8400$ pounds! Suppose the water is only up to your thighs and you try to stand in it. The above formula gives a 300-pound force on your legs. Perhaps now you will want the water to work for you and not against you. If you are going to pursue this sport you must learn properly and not just blunder in.

"Still waters run deep" and, conversely, fast waters run shallow. These are corollaries of a fundamental bit of common sense. Consider two places on the same river. Where the river is deep and wide the current is slow; and where it is shallow and narrow the current must run faster to pass the same volume of water. Once you have the feel of a stream on a particular day, you can deduce the depth from observations of width and velocity.

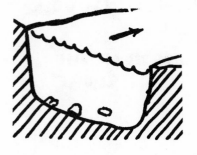

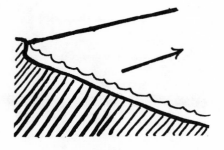

If it is slow,
it must be deep.

If it is fast and wide,
it tends to be shallow.

If it is fast yet narrow,
there may be enough depth.

The water velocity is not constant all across the river. Friction slows the water along the bottom and along the shores. It flows fastest on the surface in midstream. You must back ashore when landing or this current differential will spin your canoe about. When you swim a rapids on your back with feet downstream, you must keep your feet at the surface or the current differential will have you going head first.

WATCH THE CURRENT

DIFFERENTIALS

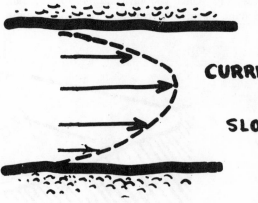

FAST
CURRENTS IN MIDDLE

SLOW NEAR THE
SHORE

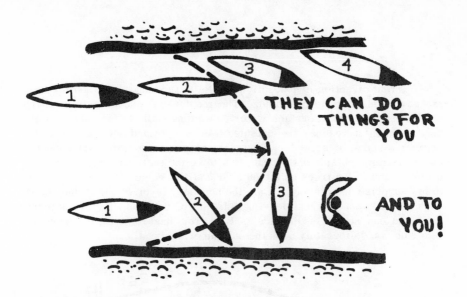

THEY CAN DO
THINGS FOR
YOU

AND TO
YOU!

Eddies are the extreme case of current differentials. Behind a large rock the current may be entirely still or even flowing gently upstream, though right beside the rock the main current rushes by at full speed. Here the current differential is abrupt; you will hear it called the eddy line or even the eddy wall. The eddy may be a welcome resting place, but you must know how to cross that sharp eddy line or you will be tipped over.

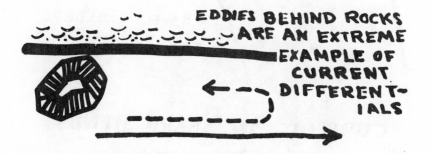

EDDIES BEHIND ROCKS
ARE AN EXTREME
EXAMPLE OF
CURRENT
DIFFERENT-
IALS

Current direction is generally parallel to the banks but when it is not, the novice may be badly fooled. The most usual exception is in sharp bends where the fast surface water flows diagonally to the outside of the bend. When it reaches the outside, it goes down and inward across the bottom, a spiraling secondary flow, leaving room for more surface water on the extreme outside of the bend. All too often there are large waves or undercut and fallen trees on the outside and the novice is swept into them to his surprise and dismay. Only the boundary layer on the inside shore does not end up at the outside. Hug this shore, perhaps with a back ferry, until you can see if the outside is free from hazards. Only at very low water do you deliberately seek the outside of the bend.

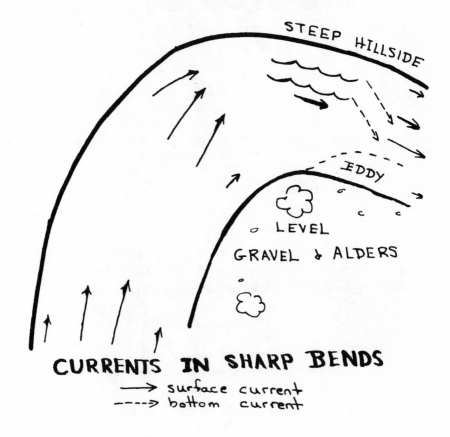

STEEP HILLSIDE

EDDY

LEVEL

GRAVEL & ALDERS

CURRENTS IN SHARP BENDS

→ surface current

----→ bottom current

Diagonal bars are often found to make the current flow across river and in general the canoe should be pointed parallel with the current to make a smaller target for rocks.

KEEP PARALLEL TO CURRENT
(EXCEPT WHEN FEARRYING)

In a turbulent rapid it may be difficult to tell when your canoe is being swept sideways and is not headed the way it is pointed. Learn to sight obstacles, be they rocks, waves, bridge piers, or tips of fallen trees, against the background. If the alignment stays unchanged, you are on a collision course. Change your plan.

IF IN ANY DOUBT OF TRUE HEADING,
KEEP SIGHTING AGAINST BACKGROUND.

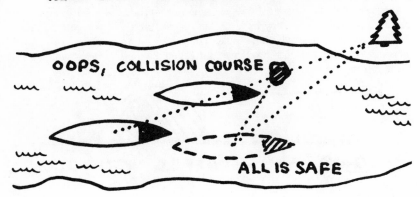

When the water meets a solid ledge it is turned aside, and that water will help to carry your canoe clear also. However, when the water goes on through the obstacle, beware. Sometimes it is pouring over a ledge or dam and you must be careful you are not swept over too. The most common and most dangerous example is where the water flows through the branches of a fallen tree. Watch for this on the outside of river bends. If you do not want that 8400 pound force pinning you on the branches, you had best stay clear way in advance.

A SOLID LEDGE TENDS TO FEND OFF BOTH WATER AND YOU

BUT AN OBSTACLE THROUGH WHICH WATER FLOWS IS VERY DANGEROUS!

Although rocks can be more damaging in swift water, they are also easier to spot. The waves reveal their hiding places. If the rock is close to the surface, the water follows the contour of the rock as it pours across and a raised convex pillow appears on the surface. Just remember that the pillows are stuffed with rock. As the rock is deeper, the surface wave appears further downstream until you can go right through without touching.

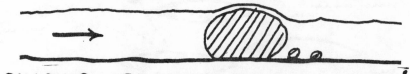

PILLOWS ARE STUFFED WITH ROCK !

IF THE WAVE IS FURTHER DOWNSTREAM OF ITS ROCK THE ROCK IS MORE SUBMERGED

IF THERE IS NO CURRENT, YOU HAVE NO WARNING

As the current becomes swifter, the pillow over the rock will be followed by one or more scalloped standing waves which are much easier to spot than the pillow. Below you will learn that such scalloped waves generally mark the channel. However, when they occur unexpectedly in a fast stretch, the bow man must look intently for that trace of a pillow at the start that says don't run these waves.

The souse hole appears behind the pillow in very powerful currents. Even when you can run over the pillow in a very large scale example, the canoe may not be able to climb out of the souse hole unless it has full forward speed (and full splash cover).

You will note that "V" pointed upstream has a rock at its tip.   A downstream "V" is nothing more than the joining of two upstream "V's"; and so it marks the course between the two rocks. The downstream "V" often has a slick and glassy appearance. It is most inviting and is usually the right course. However, it is only the route between two upstream "V's" and you must look for other signs in the turmoil after the side "V's" meet for the assurance that it is runable. Watch out for pillows.   Look for standing waves.

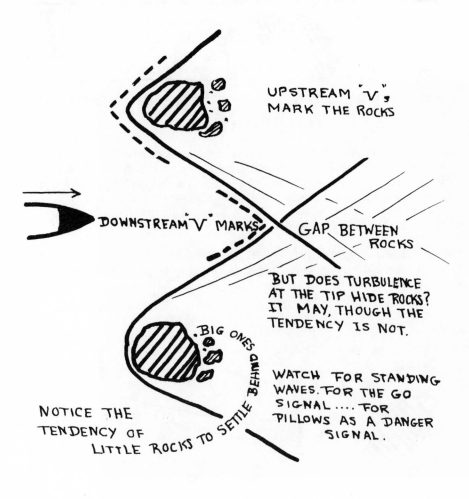

UPSTREAM "V's
MARK THE ROCKS

DOWNSTREAM "V" MARKS

GAP BETWEEN ROCKS

BUT DOES TURBULENCE AT THE TIP HIDE ROCKS? IT MAY, THOUGH THE TENDENCY IS NOT.

BIG ONES SETTLE BEHIND

WATCH FOR STANDING WAVES. FOR THE GO SIGNAL .... FOR PILLOWS AS A DANGER SIGNAL.

NOTICE THE TENDENCY OF LITTLE ROCKS TO SETTLE BEHIND

WAVES

It is the standing waves or "haystacks" that mark deep water and are the greatest delight of the canoeist. Like all river waves, these stand stationary while the water rushes through on its downstream course. They may be spotted by their characteristic scalloped shape and long length and also by the fact that they appear in groups, a half dozen or more together spaced at even downstream intervals. These waves are a vibration phen-omenon associated with the dissipation of velocity energy when a shallow, fast current reaches a deeper, slower place in the river. These waves, therefore, mark deepening water downstream of a clear path that lets the water through the rapid without dissipating its energy on the rocks. Get in line with these waves to run the ledge or rock field. Continue through the waves if they are not so big as to swamp you; otherwise draw to one side when free of the obstacles and run the waves where they are small.

SCALLOPED WAVES IN SERIES, CALLED "STANDING WAVES" OR "HAYSTACKS", SHOW DISSIPATION OF VELOCITY ENERGY WHERE WATER IS SLOWING DOWN, HENCE DEEPENING WATER.

STANDING WAVES
MARK THE CHANNEL

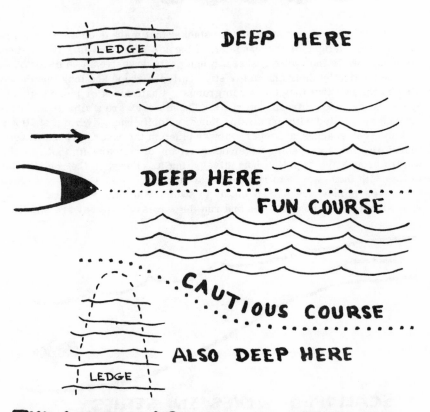

LEDGE

DEEP HERE

DEEP HERE

FUN COURSE

CAUTIOUS COURSE

ALSO DEEP HERE

LEDGE

THE WAVES ARE IN LINE WITH THE
HOLE YOU MUST COME THROUGH –
THE WATER AT THE SIDES HAS DIS-
SIPATED ITS ENERGY TUMBLING
OVER LEDGES.

There is an interesting and useful corollary to this rule. When you are in rough and turbulent water and spot a nice quiet spot, avoid it like the plague. As you shoot past, sneak a look back and you will probably see that a hidden rock with water pouring over it protects the quiet spot.

COROLLARY: BEWARE A QUIET SPOT IN THE MIDST OF GENERAL TURBU-LENCE — A SUBMERGED ROCK LIES JUST UPSTREAM.

The teacher of river canoeing will show his students pure examples of the various waves so they may learn the shapes to watch for. However, in practice these phenomena may be jumbled and harder to recognize. When you have learned this chapter, you must still train your eye. Scout from shore because you can often see rocks clearly from the side and from below though they are quite invisible from the approaching canoe. As you dodge past pillows and avoid quiet spots, look back a moment to see if they were as bad as you thought. So it is that you train your eye until you know without scouting where all the rocks are, and you have a feel for where the current is going and why. Rapids lose their look of impassable chaos and become orderly. You can relax, thrill to the water's rush and revel in the laughing waves. The rapids are yours at last.

CHAPTER 5

RIVER TACTICS

At the very heart of river canoeing are those special tactics that outwit the river and play the river currents so that they help you to place your canoe just where you want it. The steering tactic of lake canoeing is as obvious as following your nose. However, the tactics of river canoeing are not obvious; they are unexpected, and sometimes even counter to instinct. They will not be found in ordinary canoeing books; they are little known outside the white water clubs. Yet, a mastery of tactics, from full understanding to practiced skill, is the only way to make the rapids safe. Even the general canoeist should learn them early in his career before conventional maneuvers become too deeply ingrained.

STEERING IS FOR STILL WATER

Conventional steering has its place in slack or slow water. Where there is plenty of room, the stern man does all the steering and the bow man is only a galley slave. Where the channel becomes narrow and tortuous there is not room for the stern to swing wide and push the bow in a new direction. Then the bow steers his end, drawing or prying as required, usually without need of commands from the stern. However, as the current becomes swifter this practice becomes increasingly hazardous. When dodging rocks, the canoe may not be headed the way it is pointed (a characteristic not limited to pins), but will be sliding sideways. The bow may be in the water filament going to one side of the rock, the stern in a filament going to the other side. A canoe sliding sideways, even slightly sideways, makes a large target for a rock. May we remind you of the consequences of pinning canoes broadside in swift currents. Whether rock strewn rapids are "cemeteries" or "rock gardens" to you depends on your knowledge of the right tactics.

STEER (IN STILL WATER)

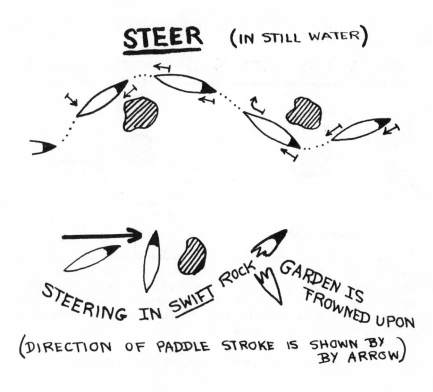

STEERING IN SWIFT ROCK GARDEN IS FROWNED UPON

(DIRECTION OF PADDLE STROKE IS SHOWN BY
BY ARROW)

PARALLEL SIDE SLIP FOR ROCK DODGING

The solution is simply to side slip the canoe. It stays parallel to the current at all times, but it slides to one side and coasts past the rock. The bow man sees the rock first and makes the decision of right or left. He draws or pries and the stern counters with the opposite stroke; a pry for a draw and a draw for a pry to move his end in the same direction. There is no need to shout. From the bow man's action the situation, though unseen, is evident. The bow man puts his end where it belongs and the stern man keeps his end directly upstream. We pointedly refute the often published statement that a canoe must have forward motion or steerageway. It is far safer to go slower relative to the rocks, to go the same speed as the water for less shipping of water in waves, to simply slide the canoe one way and the other and let it coast past the rocks. A canoe with flat bottom and shoe keel or no keel at all is obviously better here. A round bottom, a "V" bottom, or a small keel are features of lake canoes. If you will use your canoe on rivers as well as on lakes, you had best avoid these features.

PARALLEL SIDE SLIP (TO DODGE IN SWIFT ROCK GARDENS)

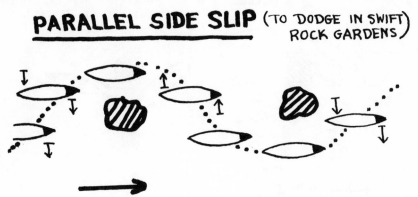

It may occur to you that a canoe is not well streamlined when moving sideways. If the problem is a long offset between the notch in a top ledge and that in a lower ledge, you will not make it by side slipping. Side slipping is, for short dodges. You aren't going to make it paddling forward either, even oversteering you will only be swept broadside over the lower ledge. You had better learn to back ferry.

BACK FERRY TO MOVE ACROSS THE STREAM

The back ferry is a vector game. The river flows in one direction, you back paddle in another direction relative to the water. Your net speed and direction relative to the rocks is the vector sum.

This is not only the way to move across stream, but also the way to put ashore without the canoe cartwheeling as it comes into the slower current. It is taught first by having the students back to shore. Next they learn to back into eddy anchors and then to cross uniform fast currents. The last and most difficult lesson is going from slack to fast water and on across a fast jet.

BACK FERRY (TO MOVE ACROSS SWIFT CURRENTS)

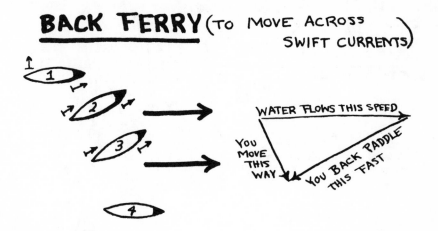

The commands of the stern man are the key. Only he sees the angle of the canoe and he directs the maneuver. The back ferry is initiated by the stern man calling "Back." Both ends back paddle to check the speed of the canoe before it reaches the rock at the head of the eddy. At the propitious moment, the stern man puts the stern toward the shore he wishes to move toward. This he does with a draw or a pry. In the latter case the canoe will pivot faster if the paddle is started under the very stern - a pryaway version of the old reverse quarter sweep. The bow is now pointed away from the shore toward which you are moving. An angle of about 30 degrees with the current is ideal. If the turbulence causes you to lose the angle, draw or pry the stern over again. If you are swept to too large an angle, command the bow to go right or left, whichever moves him toward the shore you wish to reach and straightens your angle in so doing.

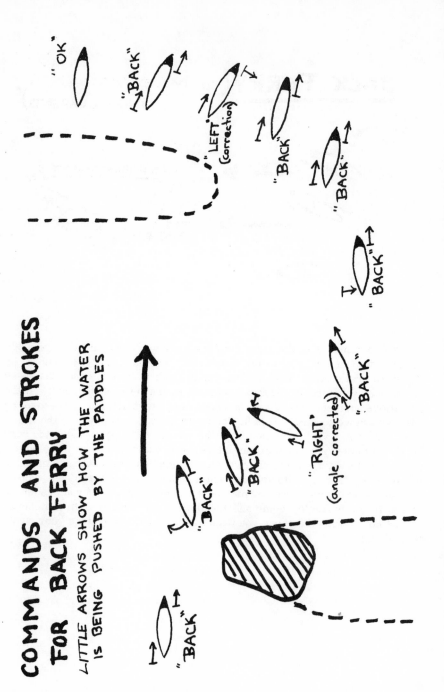

COMMANDS AND STROKES FOR BACK FERRY

LITTLE ARROWS SHOW HOW THE WATER IS BEING PUSHED BY THE PADDLES

"OK"

"BACK"

"LEFT" (correction)

"BACK"

"BACK"

"BACK"

"BACK"

"BACK"

"RIGHT" (angle corrected)

"BACK"

"BACK"

46

Some details warrant further discussion. It is often difficult to get the stern over to initiate the back ferry when you are trying to take refuge in an eddy. This is because the water deflects off the rock which causes the eddy; it is not parallel to the shore and your angle must be larger yet or you will back paddle feverishly all day without moving. To make matters worse, the bow does not experience this off-shore jet so the current is fighting your angle. You must increase your stroke power or give counter commands to your bow. That is why the reverse quarter sweep is started by prying with the paddle way under and throwing the shoulder weight into the paddle. If you are on the other tack, your draw must be more powerful. If you cannot muster enough power to get the stern over, command the bow to go the other way, away from the side you are trying to reach. It may sound like the wrong direction, but it is the only ruse that will give you the angle you need to get into the eddy.

When the student has mastered the back ferry in uniform current and going to slower current, he is ready to try backing out of an eddy into swift current. Very likely the swift current will catch the stern and spin it out and downstream. It will become an inadvertent reverse peel off without the brace and lean. After the students have wrung out their clothes, they should try again; this time side slipping the canoe until both ends are in fast water, then putting the stern ahead for the back ferry.

For lake canoes, those with keels, the back ferry is the most valuable tactic. It is very useful with shoe keel boats also. However, with the rocker bottom slalom boat it is less used. These canoes are harder to back paddle in a straight line and since they spin on a dime it is common to spin them into a forward ferry instead.

THE FORWARD FERRY

For a forward ferry you point the bow upstream and paddle forward. It is more instinctive, easier, and more powerful than the back ferry. You must first spin the boat to point upstream. The tactic is carried out with your back to the dangers downstream, and the canoe must be spun downstream again after the crossing is achieved. Of course, current differentials are used in spinning the canoe. Despite its simplicity and

47

directness, a good forward ferry from an eddy through a fast jet and into an eddy on the other side involves more skill and excitement than a back ferry. It is practiced over and over when we play a river.

The trick is to get up speed before breaking through the eddy line into the fast current. The angle must be very shallow and the speed high enough that the whole canoe is in fast current before the angle gets out of control. The result is spectacular. Not only does its momentum carry the canoe well across the fast jet, but the inertia of the canoe causes the current to push it across as it accelerates it downstream. It is a precision tactic and you must be ready to throw a quick paddle brace if the angle gets too large, until the whole canoe is in fast water and you can drive forward again.

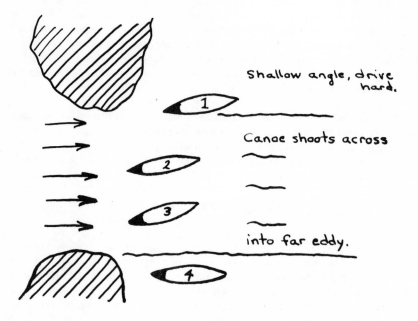

Shallow angle, drive hard.

Canoe shoots across

into far eddy.

What ferry angle is best? What angle of the canoe moves you the furthest across stream for a given slip downstream? There is a definite trigonometric solution based on the ratio of your paddling speed to the river speed.

If you can paddle	best canoe angle is	Your net direction is
7/8	30 degrees	60 degrees
1/2	60 degrees	30 degrees
1/4	75 degrees	15 degrees

of river speed.

These are optimums; any other paddling angles will give smaller net direction angle or more slip downstream. We tell beginners to hold an angle of 30 degrees. It is just perfect for being able to paddle 7/8 of river speed. If the river is slower, there is no real problem. If it is faster with waves, you may not want a bigger angle with an uncovered boat. A 30 degree angle is a good generalization. Do note that when the current is very fast you should paddle almost straight across. (Likewise a swimmer should swim straight across.)

Consider a forward ferry in a very fast jet. If your angle gets away from you, don't fight to correct it. Just drive straight across, letting the eddy on the other side turn your bow upstream again. It will look like an "S" turn and you will need a canoe lean and a paddle brace at both ends - as in an eddy turn.

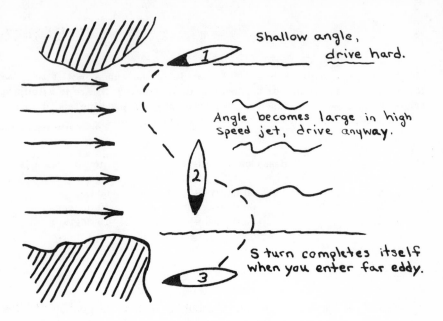

Shallow angle, drive hard.

Angle becomes large in high speed jet, drive anyway.

S turn completes itself when you enter far eddy.

FROM BACK FERRY TO EDDY TURN

The back ferry represents the cautious and cagey side of all canoeists. It is consistent with slowing down in places where you might hit rocks and slowing down to ride over large waves in an open canoe. It is absolutely necessary that you master the back paddling tactics. However, there is also a dynamic forward paddling brand of advanced white water canoeing. When the currents become powerful, the waves become large, and the souse holes yawn, then you must shift out of back paddle gear and drive forward. Drive so your momentum will carry you up the big waves lest you should slide back down into the trough or souse hole and be swallowed. If you try to back into an eddy, the current tries to pull your canoe out and onward. If you drive forward into the eddies, your momentum carries you in and the river current pushes you in. This is the eddy turn. It is then not primarily a turn, but a way of going from a powerful current into a safe eddy. The turn is a compulsory consequence. The eddy turn does not replace the back ferry; it is for different river conditions. It requires skill and much practice.

ENTERING AND LEAVING ROCK EODIES
(A) BY BACK FERRY
SAFEST METHOD, A MUST FOR ROCKY AREAS

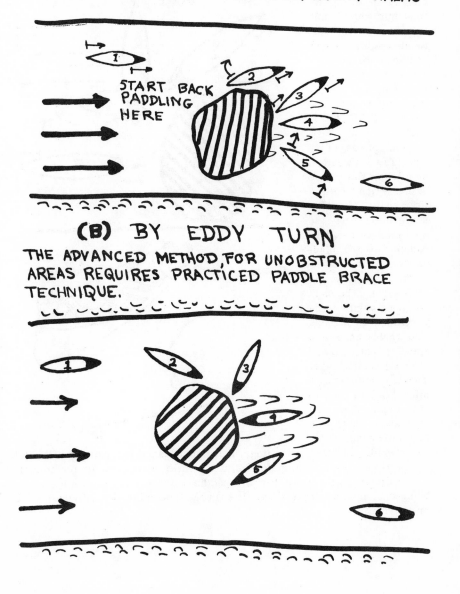

START BACK
PADDLING
HERE

(B) BY EDDY TURN
THE ADVANCED METHOD, FOR UNOBSTRUCTED
AREAS REQUIRES PRACTICED PADDLE BRACE
TECHNIQUE.

THE EDDY TURN

Suppose the stern man is paddling on the right and wants to enter an eddy also to his right. Both paddlers drive forward and the stern man gauges it so the bow knifes into the eddy just below the rock. As the bow cuts in across the eddy line the stern man leans the canoe to the right with a low brace. At the same moment the bow man slices his paddle forward, blade parallel to the keel, so his blade is in the still water. The paddle shaft points forward about 45 degrees. The whole canoe now spins quickly around the bow paddle blade. The bow man must allow his left knee to ride higher than his right so the stern can lean the canoe. The canoe skids sideward in turning. If it is not leaned far over, it will catch and be flipped to the outside of the turn. After a moment of turmoil the bow pries from the same forward paddle position, then drives forward to bring the canoe up to the rock. It's three strokes blended into one: slice, pry, drive.

If, however, the stern man is paddling on the left as they approach that right shore eddy, he must allow the canoe to be leaned by riding with his left knee high as he drives the canoe forward into the eddy. As the bow crosses the eddy line, the bow man will lean the canoe far to the right in a high brace, and hold onto the still water with a stationary draw so that the canoe will spin around his paddle blade. As the turn is completed, the bow man converts his high brace to a forward stroke and pulls the canoe up to the rock.

.Some general principles should be noted. The canoe must come from further out in the river than the eddy line and so have forward momentum toward the eddy. Both paddle forward until the bow cuts the eddy line. The person paddling on the inside of the turn braces and leans the canoe to the inside. The stern man sets up the entry point, then either low braces and leans the canoe or drives it forward. The bow man is busier: he must either slice, pry, drive or lean, high brace, turn, and drive. The stern contributes more judgment, the bow contributes more paddle skill.

53

It is the same as the eddy turn except that you are coming out of the eddy and turning down river. The principles and the bow and stern duties are the same, and the canoe lean is again to the inside of the turn.

It is interesting to compare the peel off with the advanced forward ferry because they start in much the same way but end very differently. The peel off has a large angle with the eddy line and momentum across the eddy line. The forward ferry has a very small angle and its momentum is upstream. If the ferry is into very fast water, or poorly done, the bow is swept down as in a peel off and the canoe will capsize unless it is leaned downstream and braced. The bow man should low brace for a moment, and then go back to paddling forward. However, in the peel off he wants the bow to turn downstream and uses a high brace.

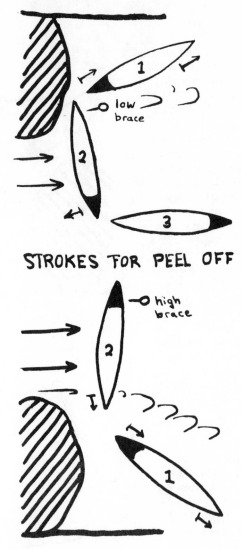

STROKES FOR PEEL OFF

PLAY THE RIVER

The tactics described above all require practice! Shorten your mileage plans, have more fun, and learn more canoeing.

CHAPTER 6

A SAFETY CODE FOR YOU

The emphasis which white water canoeists place on safety is in itself an admission of the potential hazards. The novice is sometimes scared off by being told of the tons of force from the water or the deadly numbing of ice water. We do not intentionally scare off people for we think our sport is really quite safe. We just want them to resolve at the start to be - come good white water paddlers so they will find it a safe sport.

Unfortunately, white water canoeing has a public reputation for being extremely dangerous. Every mishap of an ignorant novice makes the pa — pers from coast to coast. The public concludes that rapids are all danger- ous and that only fools venture into them. Police have been known to or- der canoeists out of rapids and motor boaters put through laws forcing us to use the same life preservers they do. We know that canoes are not tip- py, though some canoeists are. The canoe can travel in water too danger- ous for other boats. Rapids are not dangerous unless ignorant canoeists make them dangerous. If you are going to paddle white water, you owe it to yourself and to your fellow paddlers, to be a safe white water canoeist.

White water skills are the most important ingredient for white water safety. All the chapters you have read contribute to your safety and ample practice of the skills taught will help to keep you out of trouble. A later chapter will teach you what to do when you make mistakes, and another chapter helps you to develop the judgment to be a safe river canoeist. First, however, there is a safety code for you and you should learn it thoroughly.

This code was written by the expert white water boaters from coast to coast. Each word was debated and it is worthy of careful study and full adoption as your own safety code. When we read of white water fatalities we note that many of these rules were broken simultaneously - though of course the reporter did not know it - we just read between the lines. This primer can do no better than to quote verbatim the Safety Code of the American White Water Affiliation. In the appendix references there is an address where you can buy this in a little booklet to give your students and friends.

American Whitewater Affiliation

Safety Code

Adopted 1959

Revised 1963

PERSONAL PREPAREDNESS AND RESPONSIBILITY

1. NEVER BOAT ALONE. The preferred minimum is three craft.
2. BE A COMPETENT SWIMMER with ability to handle yourself underwater.
3. WEAR YOUR LIFE JACKET wherever upsets may occur. The life jacket must be capable of supporting you face up if unconscious. A crash helmet is recommended in rivers of Grade IV and over.
4. HAVE A FRANK KNOWLEDGE OF YOUR BOATING ABILITY, and don't attempt waters beyond this ability.
5. KNOW AND RESPECT RIVER CLASSIFICATION. See Section IX.
6. BEWARE OF COLD WATER AND OF WEATHER EXTREMES; dress accordingly. Rubber wet suits or long woolen underwear may be essential for safety as well as comfort.
7. BE SUITABLY PREPARED AND EQUIPPED; carry a knife, secure your glasses, and equip yourself with such special footgear, skin protection, raincoat. etc., as the situation requires.
8. BE PRACTICED in escape from spray cover, in rescue and self rescue, and in first aid.
9. SUPPORT YOUR LEADER and respect his authority.

II. **BOAT PREPAREDNESS AND EQUIPMENT (Changes or deletions at the discretion of the leader only).**

1. TEST NEW AND UNFAMILIAR EQUIPMENT before taking hazardous situations.
2. BE SURE CRAFT IS IN GOOD REPAIR before starting a trip.
3. HAVE A SPARE PADDLE, affixed for immediate use.
4. INSTALL FLOTATION DEVICES, securely fixed and designed to displace from the craft as much water as possible. A minimum of 1 cubic foot at each end is recommended.
5. HAVE BOW AND STERN LINES, **optional** for kayaks depending on local club regulations Use ¼" or ⅜" dia. and 8 to 15 ft. long rope. Fasten securely to the boat at one end and other end must release only if tugged. Floats and knots at the ends are not recommend.
6. USE SPRAY COVER WHEREVER REQUIRED; cover release must be instant and foolproof.

56

7. CARRY REPAIR KIT, flashlight, map and compass for wilderness trips; survival gear as necessary.

III. **GROUP EQUIPMENT (The leader may supplement this list, at his discretion)**
1. THROWING LINE, 50' to 100' of ¼" rope.
2. FIRST AID KIT with fresh and adequate supplies; waterproof matches.

IV. **LEADER'S RESPONSIBILITY**
1. HE MUST HAVE FULL KNOWLEDGE OF THE RIVER. He détermines the river classification on the spot and adapts plans to suit.
2. HE DOES NOT ALLOW ANYONE TO PARTICIPATE BEYOND HIS PROVEN ABILITY. Exceptions: (a) when the trip is an adequately supported training trip, or (b) when difficult stretches can be portaged.
3. HE MUST KNOW WHAT CONDITIONS IN WEATHER, VISIBILITY AND WATER TO EXPECT; he should instruct the group relative to these conditions and must make decisions on the basis of the related dangers.
4. HIS DECISIONS IN THE INTEREST OF SAFETY ARE FINAL.
5. HE DESIGNATES THE NECESSARY SUPPORT PERSONNEL, and, if appropriate, the order and spacing of boats.

V. **ON THE RIVER**
1. ALL MUST KNOW GROUP PLANS, ON-RIVER ORGANIZATION, HAZARDS EXPECTED, LOCATION OF SPECIAL EQUIPMENT, SIGNALS TO BE USED.
2. LEAD BOAT KNOWS THE RIVER, SETS THE COURSE, IS NEVER PASSED.
3. REAR-GUARD IS EQUIPPED AND TRAINED FOR RESCUE, ALWAYS IN REAR.
4. EACH BOAT IS RESPONSIBLE FOR BOAT BEHIND; passes on signals, indicates obstacles, sees it through bad spots.
5. KEEP PARTY COMPACT. Divide into independent teams if party is too big.

VI. **ON LAKE OR OCEAN**
1. DO NOT TRAVEL BEYOND A RETURNABLE DISTANCE FROM SHORE.

2. KNOW THE WEATHER. Conditions can change drastically within minutes. Beware of offshore winds.
3. SECURE COMPLETE TIDE INFORMATION for trips involving tidal currents.
4. LEAD, REAR - GUARD, AND SIDE - GUARD BOATS ARE STRONGLY RECOMMENDED to prevent large groups from becoming dangerously spread out.
5. ESKIMO ROLL mastering should be seriously considered by Kayakists on tidal or large lake waters. Canoeists should learn to right, empty of water and board a swamped canoe.

VII. **IF YOU SPILL**
1. BE AWARE OF YOUR RESPONSIBILITY TO ASSIST YOUR PARTNER.
2. HOLD ON TO YOUR BOAT; it has much floatation and is easy for rescuers to spot. Get to upstream end so boat cannot crush you on rocks. Follow rescuers' instructions.
3. LEAVE YOUR BOAT IF THIS IMPROVES YOUR SAFETY; your personal safety must come first. If rescue is not imminent and water is numbing cold or worse rapids follow, then strike for the nearest shore.
4. STAY ON THE UPSTREAM END OF YOUR BOAT; otherwise you risk being pinned against obstacles, or, in waves, may swallow water.
5. BE CALM, but don't be complacent.

VIII. **IF OTHERS SPILL**
1. GO AFTER THE BOATER; rescue his boat only if this can be done safely.

THIS SAFETY CODE HAS BEEN WORKED OUT BY THE EXPERIENCED WHITE WATER CLUBS OF THIS AFFILIATION. IT IS THE RECOMMENDATON TO BOATERS BY THE FOLDBOAT AND CANOE EXPERTS IN ALL PARTS OF THE COUNTRY. PLEASE MAKE IT A PART OF YOUR BOATING HABITS AND PLEASE HELP OTHERS TO DEVELOP THESE SAME HABITS.

CHAPTER 7

RESCUING YOURSELF AND OTHERS

In white water canoeing a few spills are inevitable. In theory, if you are very good you will never spill, but in fact you will have to do some spilling to get that good. While we look down on habitual spillers, we also lack faith in those who have never spilled. They are green troops that have never been under fire. It is better if you do spill sometime and display ingenuity and skill in getting yourself out of trouble. Even here practice is invaluable.

Never say die. Most canoes are lost not only because of an initial error, but also because of failure to do the right things afterward. It is wonderful what our canoe will weather through when we keep fighting. However, it is not blind determination alone that does it. There must be a knowledge of moves and consequences, and a mastery of skills under difficulties. It is also a flexible determination. If you cannot muster power to go right, then make the best of the left. If you are in the worst part and find yourself going backward, do a good job backward. The river will have no mercy. You must not give in.

Let us review some of the recurrent problems, starting with those of rock gardens. If you come to a grinding halt in rushing water, you must act quickly. If it is not a first class emergency, it may be your only dress rehearsal for a first class emergency. When the canoe is stationary on the rocks the water rushes against it, rises up the side, and pours in. It pours in most readily broadside, but it will also pour in the stern when in line with the current. You must quickly jump out UPSTREAM. Hold the gunwale up so water cannot come in. Lift the canoe off and hold it in the current by the stern painter so it hangs innocuously with the current, while the bow man and then you get back aboard. (It is important that you are wearing sneakers to protect your feet.)

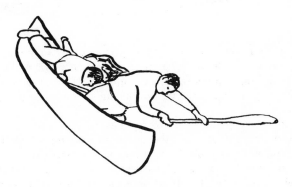

Suppose you broadside against a large boulder. Lean the canoe down stream toward the boulder, quickly, before the river climbs in and wrap the boulder in aluminum. The bow should low brace and hold the lean even shifting his paddle side to brace downstream. It is the stern who mus act now. If it is too deep or too fast to jump upstream, he might jump on to the rock. The bow would then be swept down, the canoe would pivot an go past. If the stern has the painter in his hand, he may pull the cano back into the eddy and get in. Where the rock is awash and slippery, it is better that the stern throw his weight forward so that the current can push harder on the bow and pivot the canoe around the rock.

Sometimes the bow will slide up on a rock, the canoe will stop, then swing stern downstream. It may slide free of itself or you can push free with your paddle. Don't get rattled because you are running rapids backward. Look over your shoulder – both of you. When you get to a good, big, safe eddy, do a stern first eddy turn and get straight.

When you ship water and feel it sloshing about your knees, greater care is needed that you do not roll over. Brace, backpaddle, and get into an eddy for dumping. You have much better control of your destiny while upright and with your paddles in action. If the water finally fills the canoe completely, get out even though you could stay upright. Let the canoe ride high so it is less likely to be pinned on rocks.

Once over, GET TO THE UPSTREAM END! Hand over hand along the gunwale, or scrambling right across the boat; get there fast! Otherwise you could be crushed. This is one of the most important safety rules. Perhaps your students should roll over in a safe current and find that they must stow their paddle fast to have both hands free to scramble to THE UPSTREAM END.

GET TO THE UPSTREAM END

Once at the upstream end, both of you can kick to get the canoe parallel to the current. In this way it is more likely to get through the rocks safely. Then you can try to kick the upstream end into an eddy, a sort of back ferry. If you succeed, you can salvage your own canoe.

Hold onto your canoe; the exceptions to this rule are rare. With it properly downstream of you, the canoe is your biggest and best life preserver. You will swallow less water, be easier to spot, and be a bigger target for a rope thrower. If you receive a rope, snub it at the very upstream end. Never tie it. Hold onto the free end so you can let it slip if this rescue attempt goes amiss. If, however, the water is bitter cold so you have only a minute of strength left, you should abandon all else and strike out for shore as fast as you can to save your life.

Sometime there is no choice of holding on.   You are thrown clear, or the canoe pins in and you are swept clear.   Ride on your back, feet downstream and at the surface.   If your feet drop, you may do somersaults and could hit underwater obstructions.   Slow yourself down, try to get into an eddy where you can wait for rescue.   If you have a long swim to shore in swift current, remember your swimming speed may be only a quarter or a tenth of river speed.   Swim straight toward shore without downstream or upstream component.   Do not aim for any particular rock or tree because it will soon be upstream and you must not waste energy swimming upstream. Look for a rope throw.   Hopefully it will land across your body so you can grab it before it sinks.   Be ready for a tremendous pull when the slack is gone.   Just hold on, don't tie it. You may be pulled under and have to let go.   Life preservers should be streamlined to permit faster swimming and give less drag.

SWIM ON BACK FEET FIRST ON SURFACE

When you get ashore, you may want to put on dry clothes. In freezing weather the other canoeists can usually contribute sweaters and pants from here and there. Sometimes it is better to wring out your clothes and put them back on. You can often get warm again by paddling. If you have only one set of dry clothes, save them for the end of the day.

RESCUE OF OTHERS

Everyone wants to be a hero and rescue someone, but few will practice the skills in advance to be able to do it.

Rope throw rescues are common where canoes or people are stopped by rocks and where rope throwers are posted in advance. Your throwing line should be sixty feet long. We use 3/8 inch, not for strength, but so people can hold onto it. Manila is good, but polypropylene floats, is brighter in color, and does not rot - though it is more slippery for knots and for holding on. Do not put ring buoys or even monkey fists on the end. They are too likely to be caught between rocks.

Rope throwing is well taught by the Red Cross and the Boy Scouts. A manila line should be wetted, coiled in clockwise loops, and tied in two coils to your thwart at the start of the trip. You throw one coil, the second feeds off your left hand, your foot is placed firmly on the bitter end. Be sure the free end is forward on both coils. Underhand throws give better accuracy, but bushes sometime compel a side arm throw.

The aim is all important. If your target moves with the current, you must lead it ever so slightly. The rope should fall downstream of victims, because they are looking downstream. However, it should be within arms reach so it can be grabbed before it sinks. They are less likely to miss the throw when floating on their backs with feet on the surface, or when at the upstream end of a canoe. If, however, they are on a rock, aim just upstream so the current will take the rope to them.

Belay the line quickly. When the swimmer takes hold and the river takes up the slack, there will be a tremendous pull. The rope, or the rescuer and the rope, will be dragged into the river unless a hip belay is used. Put the rope around your hips and sit down quickly where you can brace your feet. The right hand on the rope to the swimmer merely steadies it, and keeps it on the hips. It is the left hand that holds tight with the elbow straight. If the swimmer needs more line to swing around a rock, it is the left hand that lets the rope slide through, then tightens again while the elbow remains straight. This is the hip belay of the climber and it is absolutely essential.

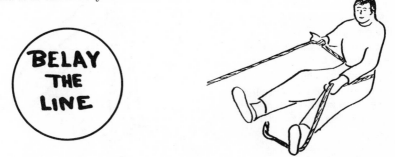

Go after people first and don't worry about their canoe until you are sure they are safe. If they are being swept down river, you will possibly chase them with a canoe. Perhaps you can take them aboard or push them into an eddy. If the water is ice cold, the rescue is not complete when you get them ashore. They may be so weak from cold as to be completely helpless. You will have to put dry clothes on them and get them warmed up with a fire, hot drink, or in any way you can devise.

Artificial respiration is hardly ever needed, but it could be terribly important. The mouth to mouth method is particularly suited to the awkward situations of river rescues and it would be wise to teach it to all your canoeists. Whoever is on the spot must start, because it may be many minutes before others can get there.

The swimming rescues taught in life saving courses are rare in canoeing. Nevertheless, canoe clubs should encourage their members to take these courses. Then, when you take a swim break at some picturesque spot, you will have your own life guards on hand.

When the people are safe, look to their canoe. You may be able to nuzzle it into an eddy, tug boat style, with your canoe. You may pick up a painter and back ferry the swamped canoe to shore. Everyone should watch for paddles floating free. Once gone, you may not catch up to them.

Canoes that have large flotation tanks at the ends can be emptied if there is just one rock where a man can stand. Otherwise, get the canoe to shallow water where a man can stand at either end and pour the water out toward shore or down stream.

If the river is wide, a canoe over canoe rescue is practical even in current and waves. The rescue canoe must be across the upstream end of the swamped canoe. The wet paddlers go hand over hand to the ends of the rescue canoe so as not to get caught downstream. The bow man of the rescue canoe keeps it perpendicular to the swamped canoe, braces it, and leans it down to help his stern man get the end of the upset canoe over his gunwale single handed. When empty, the canoe is pushed back downstream. The wet paddlers return to their canoe hand over hand (don't swim), and climb in. They must have practiced climbing in amidship and at the end, with and without their life preservers. The rescue canoe checks that they have two paddles and then backs away to give them paddling room.

Although the conventional method of climbing into a dry canoe from the water is amidship, it can also be done at the ends of an aluminum canoe. Get beside the end. Kick to get your arms on top of the tank. Kick again to get hands down, elbows up, and torso across the top of the tank. Swing your legs aboard. It's not elegant, but you don't have to move to the middle. Young people with adequate muscles find it takes less skill. Your students should practice both methods.

Salvage of canoes pinned on rocks is not uncommon. Your line is first used as a safety to get weaker members of the crew and knapsacks ashore, then to get more strong men out to the wreck. If the water is not too deep, they can stand in a row and lift the upstream gunwale up.

If this is not feasible, fish up a free flowing painter with your paddle and tie a line to it. If heavy pulling will be required, painter rings, seats, and thwarts are going to pull loose. Here you will need a rope sling around the end most likely to be moveable. This is generally the end not fully submerged, the end most upstream, or the end closest to the rock. Now get your manpower ashore for the pull. You will pull it upstream or up in the air, such that the pull of the water on that end of the canoe is ever less until the water swings the canoe around the rock and into the eddy below. You can retrieve it with the line made fast to the painter. You may not be able to pull it free. Some clubs carry a "come along" or other form of block and tackle. The snap rings or carabiners of the rock climber can be used as pulleys to gain a mechanical advantage. Lacking such equipment, you can try tying your line to a stout tree. When you push or pull sideways at the center of the line, there is a tremendous end force. By using two such lines, you can take up the slack in one while pulling sideways on the other. The canoe moves only a little each time.

You may decide to tie your painter line to a tree and come back when the water is lower. The forces will be very much less. Sometimes the rocks will have chewed mouse holes in the canoe, or the canoe may be missing altogether.

First aid kits are in order for man and canoe. A waterproof kit could be strapped to the thwart of one canoe. Cuts and scratches are most likely, but broken bones, burns, even snakebites might be possible.

Canoes may also need first aid before continuing. An aluminum canoe can often be pushed back into shape by putting it on a grassy spot and all standing in it. There may be tears and pulled rivets. Waterproof adhesive tape, from your "man" kit, will stop the leaks and last out your trip. When you get home, rivet on aluminum patches. Don't weld. A fiber glass canoe can also be patched temporarily with adhesive tape. On long trips you should also carry glass cloth, resin, and catalyst.

You will learn a lot more about rescues as you gain experience in white water canoeing. They are very common, so the word "rescue" is over dramatic. It's just a daily occurrence and part of the fun.

CHAPTER 8

STRATEGY ON THE HYPOTHETICAL RIVER

It is an artificiality to have divided river canoeing into strokes, water reading, and tactics. In real life there is no separation of these skills for they are inextricably interwoven. In this chapter we shall try to show you the integrated pattern. We call it the strategy of river canoeing.

With your fine equipment, your mastered strokes, and your practiced tactics you are still only a chip on the water unless you can blend them all into a plan of action. You had best get running practice with an experienced group. We happen to be taking a trip down the Hypothetical River and if you care to join us we would be pleased. This is no ordinary river; ordinary rivers start steep and fast and end large and placid. The Hypothetical River is at first a gentle meandering stream, of only Grade I. It becomes steeper and as side streams add water it becomes more and more powerful. The canyon at the end is generally rated Grade IV.

This bridge is the put-in point. The leader studies the river from the bridge. There is a riffle in sight and he can see that the stream is neither in flood nor too shallow to carry the canoes through. He has permission to park cars in the clearing and directs that canoes be launched beside the bridge. Your car  has already been dropped off at the take out, and since there we have had three canoes on each car. Be sure to bring your car keys with you! All hands are busy carrying canoes, strapping on kneepads, and tying the spare paddles in with breakable twine. The crews climb in and push off as they are ready, but wait right there in the eddy making minor adjustments to knee straps. The leader has already checked the pairing off and has separated a young couple who lack experience. He checks over the equipment and notes that all have life jackets. Everyone will wear life jackets, experts too, for they must set an example and also be ready for rescues. (This rule may be waived by the leader on gentle streams in warm weather.) Everyone knows the trip leader's word is law; it must be so. He appoints Bob to lead and Don to sweep. While Don wets the throwing line and ties it in two coils to his thwart, the lead reminds everyone that they must keep the canoe BEHIND in sight at all times. Then you are off.

You are paddling bow with me and we pull out in third place. I try my commands on you: "Right, left, back, forward." If I am sure you can follow orders quickly and well, I feel I can get you through. At first the course is narrow and winding, so you are constantly drawing and prying to get the bow around without the stern having to get in the bushes trying to steer the canoe. The canoeing requires no words and we are discussing the greenness of the forest. It is so lush that when we come to a fallen tree there is no chance of carrying around. We all stay clear and one at a time the canoes come in perpendicular to the trunk. They climb onto the log and lift the canoe across between them quickly before the current can swing it broadside. The stream is so tortuous that we see only one canoe in front and one behind. The canoe in front shouts "two," I shout "three" and the count goes back "four," "five," "sweep," "five," "four." You catch on and shout "three." The lead canoe is reassured that no one has committed the cardinal sin of letting the canoe behind get out of sight.

The stream becomes wider and shallower. We come into a sweeping bend to the right. Typically, the left bank is steep and wooded, the right shore is flat gravel with scraggly alders. Our lead coasts into the bend, knowing we should come out on the outside, but letting the river current decide our path down to the outside of the bend. We coast along the outside only three feet from shore and duck through branches of leaning trees. You reach for a branch to pull yourself right and I correct you. We try to be tactful, but some things get us excited. Don't ever hold onto tree branches. When you pull from above the water surface, it will upset you. Put your paddle in the water and pull all you want. The canoe ahead runs up on a rock and swings broadside to block the only passage. I grab a tree branch directly behind me. Canoeing is full of exceptions.

We standardize on the one best way to do each thing. We do things in that one best way by habit, while our mind gropes with other problems. Sometimes we deliberately, and for good reason, do something differently. I always kneel, except when I sit or stand. For guiding the canoe put all your faith in your paddle strokes. Don't coast into trouble and try to fend off the rocks. If you do get in five powerful strokes and you are still going to hit the rock, I would be understanding if you fended off at the water line.

There is a sharp drop off ahead and they are landing to look it over. The lead canoe sneaks very close by the shore to his landing point and so do we. (A club member who didn't think this was important once went over a dam sideways.) We join the group who are looking at a five foot drop across a ledge that slopes down about forty five degrees and we find the lead explaining his diagnosis. If there were standing waves below he would not worry about running it, because if the boats did spill they would be washed downstream and could be fished out without difficulty. Instead there is a hydraulic jump.

Standing Waves

Hydraulic Jump

69

Our lead illustrates the back flow on the surface by throwing in a piece of wood. It floats upriver and is trapped in the trough where it tumbles and tumbles. He is afraid the canoes might ground on the ledge and their bows be swept back to dump them in the trough. Or, they might swamp plunging into the hydraulic jump. In either case, they would be trapped and tumbled like the piece of wood. The only escape would be to swim out the end or to get rid of your life jacket and dive down to get in the downriver current. He directs us to carry our canoes.

SOME CAN'T RESIST RUNNING DAMS

STANDING WAVES SHOW DOWNSTREAM CURRENT ON SURFACE – GO AHEAD BUT SLOWLY, YOU MAY SWAMP.

IF THERE IS NOT ENOUGH WATER, THINGS COME TO AN ABRUPT HALT.

DANGER ! HYDRAULIC JUMP INSTEAD OF STANDING WAVES SHOWS BACKFLOW

IF YOU STOP YOU WILL QUICKLY BE SWEPT INTO THIS POSITION, YOU MAY HAVE TO ABANDON CANOE AND SWIM DOWN TO ESCAPE !

At a diagonal gravel bar, the lead notes where the current runs out most strongly below. In line with that point he swings his canoe perpendicular to the bar and slows it down lest it scrape. On either side the dancing ripples are dark, a sign that they will not float a canoe. The lead side slips to deliberately graze the biggest boulders knowing the water is deeper next to them. His bow is using a cross draw instead of a pry for this shallow water. The fourth canoe cuts the corner and grounds, and canoe five follows him. Both get their feet wet. If you can't smell your way through thin water, you should meticulously follow someone who can.

After the forks we run a rock garden, about Grade II. You pick our course from the bow and I keep the stern in line with the current. One boat whacks an obvious rock with its stern; the bow drew clear but the stern saw he was pointed free - a lake canoeist no doubt. Ahead we see the white of waves, but the river narrows so there is ample depth. The lead runs along the edge, between Scylla and Charybdis, back paddling to help the bow rise over the crests. He back ferries into the eddy below where the others join him one by one. The canoe that whacked the rock, however, overshoots the eddy; they don't think it matters. Our lead reprimands them.

ANN SIMON

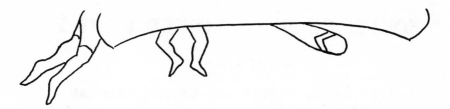

In the next rock garden we play eddy anchor. The lead back ferries into a tiny eddy, just touches the rock, and then pushes on to let the next canoe come in. This practice is appreciated when we see the ledges below. The first drop is runable on the right, but the only place where scalloped waves mark a break in the lower ledge is on the left. It is a real challenge to a back ferry, and the lead suggests that the two weakest crews portage. They do.

At Big "S" bend, the lead anticipates trouble and sneaks along the very inside of the first bend. The water has become more powerful. Where the rocks force him out, he back ferries in again. One canoe gets out too far and is caught in the diagonal surface flow. He sees the tree toppled out into the waves on the outside of the bend. He then sights the tip of the tree against the shore, realizes he is on a collision course, and steepens his back ferry angle until the canoe is almost perpendicular to the shore (about parallel to the tree trunk). Luckily only his bow hits a glancing blow and his canoe is spun the rest of the way. He is now going stern first and should be able to make the eddy on the inside of the second bend. However, the bow man becomes rattled running the waves backward and misses his lean and brace when the stern crosses the eddy line. The lead boat has already done a forward ferry to the inside of the second bend and he fishes them out.

ROUTE CHOICE – LINKED BENDS

HIGH WATER

STAY NEAR INSIDE OF BEND: BEWARE OF FALLEN TREE.

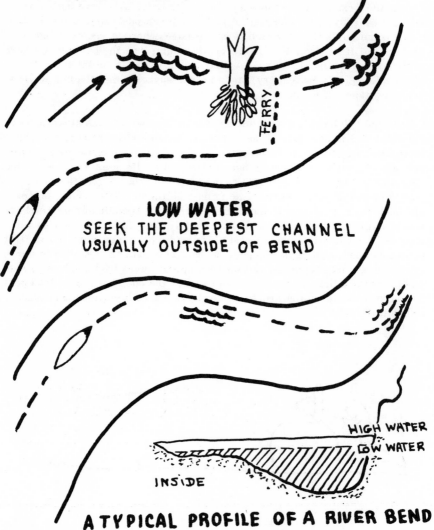

LOW WATER

SEEK THE DEEPEST CHANNEL USUALLY OUTSIDE OF BEND

FERRY

HIGH WATER
LOW WATER

INSIDE

A TYPICAL PROFILE OF A RIVER BEND

I should warn you about flood water on this river. At the start the trip leader studied the river from the bridge before he gave the word to unload and launch. If there had not been enough water flowing to carry boats through such riffles, he would have changed his put-in to a point downstream. If it had been in flood, he would have shifted to another river - unless of course the trip had been billed as expert and other applicants had been turned down. The dangers of flood water are swifter and more powerful currents - doubling the speed quadruples the forces. These currents can sweep canoes under fallen trees and into big waves. Multiple swampings are likely and only splash covered canoes can chase after them. Flood water flowing through standing trees is particularly dangerous.

Lunch break is on the right bank below the ledges. There are woods here (girls upstream, boys downstream) and it is also a good place to play the rapids. The leader posts two rope throwers at the bottom of the schuss and the swimmers come through with their life jackets on, feet forward. The weather is not what other people call swimming weather, but canoeists are used to it and dressed for it - long johns or wet suits. Two canoes work on forward ferries while the rest of us relax and talk.

A young fellow asks advise about taking teen agers on extended northwoods trips, and is deluged. Take as little duffel as possible; added weight makes a canoe less maneuverable and more likely to swamp. Even so, portage the duffel at major rapids. You should be able to portage it on one load, then scout the rapids on the return. Sometimes the canoes are run single to save any risk of swamping. In any case, you are much more cautious on wilderness trips because you can't risk losing canoes. Another major point is that time should be spent playing the river to develop white water skills. The bottoms of big rapids are safe places and the canoes are still unloaded. Why not pitch camp right there and spend the whole afternoon? It is an investment in safety besides being fun.

After lunch we come to three low scrubby islands in the middle of the river (diagram on following page). The river curves right against a hillside just below, and the current runs between the islands making a rapid between each. At low water there would be no question that we take the first runable rapid to the left and get on the outside of the bend, the low side where more and more water will come between the islands to join us. At flood water, we would hug the right shore and run or portage the last

ISLANDS

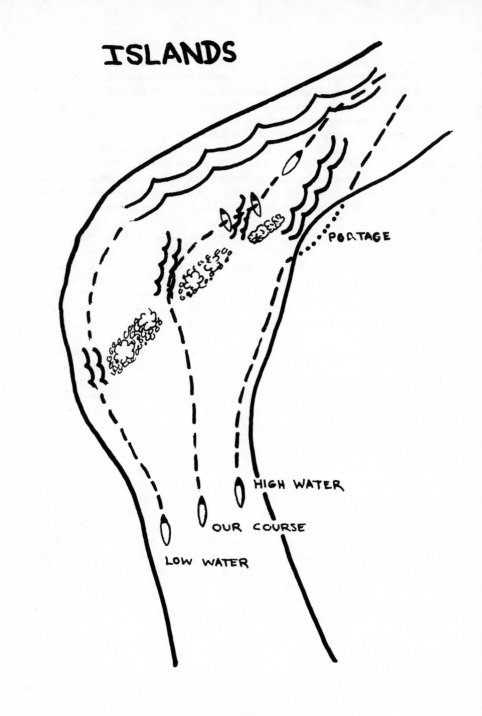

PORTAGE

HIGH WATER

OUR COURSE

LOW WATER

opening. Today the water level is moderate. The lead elects the second channel only to find the other two are also runable. We back ferry through the jet from the third break, then run out the waves where the jet from the fourth channel meets the outside of the bend. Everyone makes it, but all except the lead and sweep have to stop and dump water. It isn't safe to paddle with water sloshing in the bottom of your canoe.

We put ashore at the head of Imaginary Canyon and here our two weakest crews drop out to take the shuttle car back. Here we put the full splash covers on the aluminum canoes. The fiber glass canoes have needed their spray skirts all afternoon. There is anticipation and excitement as equipment is made just exactly right. We check the feel of our knee straps, try a few braces, and then the four boats peel off in quick succession.

Waves can now be taken in stride, but there are enormous boulders with water pouring over them, into deep souse holes that are followed by immense stopper waves. We guess which filament of water passes clear and get in that filament as far ahead as possible. We find ourselves paddling across stream, running through waves sideward. There is an occasional quick back ferry to keep away from rock outcroppings along the cliffs on the outside of corners. However, we must charge forward every time we see a stopper in our path, and we do much driving forward and oversteering. If we have enough momentum, we may brace for an instant at a critical spot, as where we hit a big wave with only the right side of our boat. Mostly we drive, and throw the braces on an emergency basis. After each tough one, the lead canoe dives into an eddy to see everyone through. He makes sure they are all set, no water seepage around spray skirts to be bailed, before peeling off again.

The cars are at the take out beach as we charge down the last row of scallops and dive into the final quiet eddy with the thunder of the canyon receding behind us. It has been a splendid thundering finale. Who is to say it is any more beautiful than the serene movement of morning or the lively scherzo of midday? All are part of canoeing.

CHAPTER 9
TEACHING RIVER CANOEING

The following ideas are set down as a preliminary guide to instructors. The suggested teaching outline is intended to cover the following:

    (1)   Pre-school assigned reading

    (2)   About 10 hours of class instruction on the river with a student/instructor ratio no greater than 6/1

    (3)   About 5 hours of lecture and discussion

It is assumed that all students hold an American Red Cross Basic Canoeing Certificate, or the equivalent in experience, and are perfectly at home in a canoe.

The objective of this discussion is to help any organized canoeing group conduct classes without outside assistance. The general concepts underlying the program are:

    (1)   Cover the fundamentals in logical order and in a minimum time.

    (2)   Teach the most effective and reliable techniques.

    (3)   Instructors are to explain, demonstrate and drill students in their practice.

    (4)   No student will become a proficient river canoeist during this short program. Therefore, the program must be supplemented with a few years experience, practice, and association with experienced groups.

PRE-SCHOOL ASSIGNED READING

Ideally, the instruction staff should supply recommended reading matter selected to introduce the new concepts and to answer in a general way the basic how, when, and where questions. It is suggested that short write-ups be supplied on the following:

        Equipment and clothing
        Paddle strokes for rivers
        Reading the water
        Tactics and strategy
        Safe practice: safety code, self rescue, rescuing others
        Trip leading and group cruising
        Some guide information on local streams

RIVER INSTRUCTION AND PRACTICE

Before putting canoes in the water, discuss the importance of TEAM PLAY. Make sure students understand that the group proceeds single file, with an agreed spacing between canoes, and that each crew has responsibilities to the whole group. Discuss the techniques used to launch and land canoes in currents. Make sure every pack and spare paddle is properly stowed and secured.

The first job on the water is to quickly review and then perfect the basic strokes. Find a quiet spot, review and practice them in their order of importance to river canoeing: back stroke, draw, pryaway, paddle brace, reverse sweeps, cross draw, and forward. Work to make these strokes as effective as possible. Mention the possibilities of combination strokes.

Just as the music student wants to progress beyond the scales as soon as possible, your students will want to push off down river to see what's beyond the bend. Before you do, explain, demonstrate, and practice bow and stern stroke coordination in back paddling, parallel movements, and back ferrying. These maneuvers will be brand new to most students, so be sure to explain when they are used and why the current makes them necessary. After some practice (don't expect perfection) you are ready to shove off down river into a short section of easy going with no frightening situations. Here you can practice on fundamentals without endangering your group. The instructor will probably take the stern of the lead canoe suggesting to those that follow at regular intervals, a follow the leader technique. For example: the instructor back ferries to the right. He stops near the bank and watches each crew do the same back ferry. He comments on the proficiency of each crew, making suggestions for improvement.

As the group moves downstream practicing, the instructor, leading the group, makes any exercise possible out of every rock, fallen tree, bend, wave, and ripple so his students can get experience beyond the actual rating of this stretch of stream. He may, on occasion, paddle back upstream and run a particular stretch again, showing how to seek out the weaker currents and play the eddies to get back up.

You may find yourself getting a little hoarse. If so, it's probably because you have been shouting at your group a bit too much and too loudly.

Your job is to make your comments simple and clear; phrase them carefully so you won't confuse.

After an hour or two, the group will begin to grasp these fundamental coordination maneuvers. At this point, it is well for the instructor to take a new student into his canoe every 20 or 30 minutes. This provides the opportunity for individual coaching. The following would be a typical coaching period.

With the student in the bow, quickly review his stroke effectiveness. Follow this with back paddling, parallel movement, and back ferry. Give commands even if there are no obstacles to help the student increase his rapidity of reaction. During this time the instructor can discuss and point out some of the elements of water reading; selecting the proper course with respect to obstacles, waves, and eddies.

The instructor then moves the student into the stern and repeats the review of stern strokes, coordinated movements from the stern man's point of view, and the stern man's responsibility for selecting the general course: right or left shore, rapids' entry point, and the overall plan of action. Meanwhile, all other crews in the class are still playing follow-the-leader. This general plan requires that the other students in the class change partners too, thus assuring that some weak student doesn't get the idea he is being completely successful when perhaps it's just that he has an exceptionally capable partner. If the class is large and has two instructors, the second instructor should be stern man in the last canoe. He can change places at intervals with students in the last half of the procession and can explain the first instructor's demonstration runs to the class.

When the rapid ahead is long, or perhaps a bit more difficult, the instructor is advised to land and examine the rapid with the class. A discussion of the route through and the strategy required follows. The instructor can then demonstrate the best way to run it, land at the bottom and while the next crew goes through, discuss the good and bad points of each run with the rest of the class. It may be desirable for each crew to carry or track their canoes back upstream and run the same rapid a second time.

The instructor must realize that the students will tire more quickly than he. Occasional rests in eddies will provide opportunities to point out water reading examples. Give your students plenty of opportunity to ask questions. It will show you the areas that need more explaining. Use lunch period to discuss safety precautions and rescue methods.

With proper planning and selection of river sections to run, the above practice can be gotten from a section of river 4 to 6 miles long, certainly no longer and perhaps much shorter. For the second day's river work, try to find a more challenging stretch of river. Begin the second day's work with a drill in the coordinated maneuvers of back ferries, parallel movements, and back paddling in stronger currents. Continue to play follow-the-leader. Stop and discuss any rapid that will serve to illustrate points about water reading, tactics, or strategy. Ask the students to give their ideas on how it should be run, both as to general course to follow and the maneuvers they expect to need to run it that way. Once again, the instructor and partner go first to demonstrate; they land, return to the watching group and comment as the other crews go through. (With two instructors, the lead can simply wait at the bottom and discuss the runs with the group as they accumulate.) On the second day, particularly, it may prove very valuable to run some of the best rapids two or more times. This is a good confidence builder.

On the second day you will tackle the eddy turn, paddle brace, and such. While you are practicing for perfection here, be sure they do not forget or discard the back ferry which is not an instinctive maneuver. Revert to it occasionally to be sure they are able to "shift gears."

In teaching paddle brace, emphasize that one puts his trust in the paddle at all times. Tell them you do not want to see hands holding onto the gunwales in a crisis; the knees hold the canoe. Put the paddle in the water and use it. In classes where canoes are deliberately upset, have one partner try to upset, the other resist with paddle braces. That way, when it does go over it will be a surprise. They will have to collect their wits, stow their paddles, and get to the upstream end.

Crews are rotated on the second day as on the first. During individual coaching periods, the instructor now lets his student pick the course, both from the bow and the stern. Unless some real danger seems imminent, follow his suggestion. If it works, it will do wonders for his confidence; if it doesn't everyone will profit by the mistake. You may even have an opportunity to demonstrate some of the self-rescue techniques.

The emphasis the second day is on the tactics and strategy of running safely, and making the current work for you. Give particular effort to student understanding of ways to determine their motion relative to obstacles. Be sure to distinguish between methods used to navigate bends in the river when: (a) You don't know the river; (b) You know the river, but the water is heavy; and (c) You know the river and the water is low.

If weather permits, purposely get into some difficulties that will permit demonstration of self-rescue techniques; at the very least discuss them and demonstrate them, on dry land if necessary. Practice rope throwing at floating canoes, even though they may not need help. The thrower will get some appreciation of how his throw must lead the moving canoe in order to hit it amidship or aft, and the stern man of the target canoe will learn how to snub it to avoid upsetting. Discuss and demonstrate, if possible, ways of rescuing canoeists stranded on rocks in midstream; also ways of retrieving "hung-up" canoes. Try to end the second day on the river with some really good rips so that all your students will leave wishing for more.

Rescue practice, like fire drills, should be as realistic as possible. It is best to have them swim a rapid with life preservers after posting two or more rope throwers. They get accustomed to swimming rapids and they learn the importance of rope throwing accuracy and practice. Tell them that such practice is a worthwhile and fun feature of any canoe trip. An upset canoeist is often too rattled to remember to get to the upstream end. Deliberate upsetting in an unobstructed rapid with a rope thrower at the bottom should increase their safety in the future.

As an instructor, your students will be following your example. Be sure that your own performance justifies their trust. If you make a mistake yourself, point it out to the class rather than run the risk of letting them start a bad habit. Try to know the whys about everything you say and do. Avoid dogmatism. If something doesn't seem right, discuss it with your class and try to arrive at a better way. Some students will require more individual instruction. Give it to them either with an extra period in your canoe, or by thoughtful selection of relatively skilled partners whom you believe will have the tact to help them.

EVENING LECTURE AND DISCUSSION PERIODS

After one day of experience on the river, your students will more readily understand the written material given them beforehand. A more thorough coverage of this material through lectures, slide talks, movies, flannel-board discussions, etc. is very much in order. Follow the same subject headings as used in the handout material. Organize these sections so the students have an opportunity to ask questions. Try to have exhibits of equipment for them to look at. Plan to take some steps forward on new phases of the subject such as "Canoe Camping." End each discussion with something having inspirational value. Finally, be sure they understand that to continue to grow they must associate themselves with groups and individuals with more experience than they have. Tell them about the available associations, individual clubs, available literature, and where to acquire the necessary equipment.

To your surprise, you will find that all your preparations and the execution of a teaching plan will vastly increase your own understanding of the subject.

Some of your teaching aids, such as movies, slides, film loops, and flannel board, must be worked out for yourself. Some can be obtained elsewhere.

The American Whitewater Affiliation training film may be rented via Paul McElroy, 65 Old Concord Road, Belmont, Massachusetts 02178. It is 16mm in color and is accompanied by a separate tape which requires a tape recorder for playback.

Film loops are sections of movie film four to eight feet in length, with the end spliced to the beginning so they show a single well done tactic over and over. Sets of such loops should become available for white water tactics and slalom techniques, for both canoe and kayak, in 8 and 16mm. We appreciate being given film footage that is suitable. When we are satisfied with each set, copies will be sent to the AWA Safety Committee. Loops should show a variety of seasons, canoe types, equipment, and water situations along with a basic tactic done to perfection, so no errors are seen even after many loops through the projector. The Buck Ridge Loops may be borrowed until the others are available. Study the sheets sent with the loops. Run them just right so they do not kink and break. Learn the many points that each loop is to illustrate.

A flannel board about 4 feet by 8 feet is about right. Sew or paint the river boundaries - a big "S" bend can be used for almost any situation. Canoes, waves, rocks, current arrows, "V's", fallen trees, etc. are cut from cardboard.   A visual aids store can provide the prickly backing that holds them to the flannel.

Safety Codes of the American Whitewater Affiliation may be bought in quantity from Harold Kiehm, 2019 Addison Street, Chicago, Illinois 6 0 618, for four dollars ($4.00) a hundred.

This manual is available at discount for large quantities.

The "Instructor's Check List" below may help you remember the points you want to cover on the river. Make up some copies and carry one in your pocket.

INSTRUCTOR'S CHECK LIST

Safe Practice:
        Check Safety Equipment
        Explain Group Running Rules
        Safety Code - go over it

Check and Improve Strokes

Back	Cross Draw	Reverse Quarter Sweep
Draw	Forward	Low Brace
Pryaway	J Stroke	High Brace

Bow-Stern Team Play
        Bow and Stern responsibilities
        Commands: Back, Forward, Right, Left, O. K.

Tactics for Moving Water
        Parallel Movement
        Back Ferry: Into eddy, right and left
        Forward Ferry: Both paddling sides in both directions
        Back Ferry: From one eddy to another

Reading the Water
> Current Differentials, show canoe spin
> Width, Velocity, Depth Relationship
> Current Direction: diagonal bars and bends
> Upstream and Downstream "V's"
> Rocks, Pillows, Souse Holes, Shallows
> Motion Relative to Obstacles - sighting beyond
>> Standing Waves   Hydraulic jumps

Strategy - Making a Plan of Action
> River Bends: Heavy Water - Low Water
>> (be careful on new rivers)
> Eddies: Stern first or bow first?
> Standing Waves: Run them or avoid them?
>> Back, Brace, or Forward?

Advanced Tactics
> Eddy Turns: Both paddling sides in both directions
>> The Draw Brace   Slice, Pry, Drive
>> Canoe Lean
> Peel Off: Both paddling sides in both directions
>> Peel off vs. forward ferry - angle

OOPS!
> Ship Water: Balance and back paddle to eddy
> On Rock: Lean downstream, keep upstream gunwale up
> Swamp: Get out, hold on, stow paddle
> Capsize: Hold on, stow paddle, upstream end
> Swim: On back, feet downstream at surface
> WORK INTO EDDY!

Rescue
> Save People First!
> Rope Throw: the Throw, the Aim, the Belay
> Snubbing on Canoe
> Canoe over Canoe - river style
> End Tank and other dumps
> Watch for Paddles
> Salvage: Don't take chances saving equipment!

CHAPTER 10

SLALOM CANOES ARE DIFFERENT

This book is written for the masses of ordinary canoeists who run rivers for fun and recreation. These include the clubs, family groups, camp expeditions, scout troops and explorer posts. Because of their numbers, these people are the most important part of canoeing and they gain the most health and happiness from running the rivers. In addition to these people, however, there is a class of experts. They run spectacular rivers and display their skill in slaloms. They are the inspiration of younger paddlers, and they develop better equipment and techniques. They are in the public eye and bring prestige to canoeing. They paddle the slalom canoes.

Slalom canoes are the fiber glass white water specials that have evolved in canoe slalom. They are the C-1 and C-2, the one and two man canoes, and the K-1 or one man kayak. They are often elliptical in cross section and completely decked over with cockpits for the paddlers, who are sealed in with spray skirts. They often have a rocker bottom so they may be turned more easily. This, along with the rounded ends and elliptical cross section has won them the unofficial name of "Banana Boats."

Some who read this book will go on to slalom canoes. All may encounter statements that apply to slalom canoes but do not apply to handling ordinary canoes. It seems important, therefore, to devote one chapter to explaining the marked differences in handling the special white water fiber glass canoes that we are referring to here as slalom canoes.

The slalom canoe is narrower and rounder in the bottom so that it seems much less stable to the beginner. Surprisingly enough, the very features that make it more tippy in flat water make it less susceptible to heavy waves. It rolls and pitches less, and the waves have less grip to throw it over. However, it requires considerable body agility and balance, as well as effective paddle bracing. Only in the hands of the expert does the slalom canoe become the safer one in rough water.

The lack of any keel and the rocker bottom make this canoe more difficult to paddle in a straight line in quiet water. However, the keel-less rocker bottom makes it much more maneuverable, easier to turn when you want, and easier to hold straight when the water wants to turn you. Again, it will cause the beginner trouble, but will do amazing things in the hands of the expert.

These different characteristics call for use of different tactics. The deck and spray skirts remove the danger of swamping the canoe (but not of capsizing) in heavy waves. This makes it unnecessary to sneak around big waves and, in fact, it is generally desirable to drive forward aggressively through these waves which might otherwise stop the canoe and cause it to broach or capsize. The great maneuverability and ease of turning these canoes can be used to great advantage. Side slips and back ferries may be used on occasion, but they are difficult in heavy water where forward speed is needed to break through waves and holes. Consequently, the back ferry is little used. The common tactic for moving across the current is to turn and drive forward to the desired filament of water, or even to eddy turn and forward ferry across. However, those of you who are paddling aluminum canoes with standard (rather than shoe) keels had best stay with the back ferry.

Because of the low inherent stability and the extreme tumble-home of these canoes, extreme leans are both desirable and necessary when man-euvering through strong current differentials. Without them you will be flipped over. If you will exercise the right lean, a strong paddle brace and a good sense of balance, these canoes will perform violently rapid eddy turns and ferry across amazingly fast jets of water. Some current models have no tumble-home and so require less lean.

A play-the-river tactic that becomes possible with these decked canoes is surfing diagonally across the upstream slopes of large waves in fast currents. The canoe coasts down the upstream face of the wave, bow upstream, fast enough to match the downstream current of the river. With skill you can go back and forth across the wave without paddling - only bracing. Such skill takes practice.

The slalom canoe provides plenty of upsets while learning. It saves time and danger, and also develops correct reactions if you will roll back upright with your paddle. There is, therefore, good reason to learn first the most difficult skill of all, the Eskimo roll.

The Eskimo roll is a challenge to teacher and student alike. Physical strength is important when learning, but not so important when the skill is mastered. Physical coordination must be good for this complex maneuver that involves the whole body. There is an understanding problem because the spectator sees the demonstrator roll around; the boater sees and feels the world turning about him. The transition from observing to doing is very confusing. Only the capable and determined paddler should take up rolling.

The teaching challenge comes from the inability of the watcher to see underwater details of the demonstration, from lack of words to describe the motions, and from difficulty of seeing what the student does wrong. Once the student has done a successful roll, he can usually do another. The memory is in his muscles. However, to learn the other hand roll, you must go back to the beginning. The mind knows how and the muscles don't. The teaching challenge is to get the student somehow to do a good roll. Here is about the way it goes.

The place should have clear water and be about four feet deep. The water should be warm as the instructor spends a long time in it. Rolling classes are good off-season club activities, indoors in the winter, outdoors in the summer. You need an easily rollable slalom canoe with knee straps and foot braces, preferably a C-1. However, a C-2 with the front cockpit covered will do.

The description that follows is for a right hand roll. That is, the paddle is held as when paddling on the right, and the paddler comes up on the right of the canoe so it is actually a counterclockwise roll. At the start it will help if all your students are learning the same direction. They will get more out of watching the others practice; until they learn the other direction they will have to find a C-2 partner who rolls the same way.

First you demonstrate the roll emphasizing that you bring the canoe up with knees and hips and that you leave your face in the water until the very last. Put the first student in the canoe without a paddle and stand in the water on his right side. Have him take hold of your wrists which you hold about at the water surface. Have him put his face in the water first. Then, as a separate motion, roll the canoe toward you beyond its stability point, then back. Soon he will be going all the way over and back up. At first students pull their body up and can't make the boat follow. They must learn to bring the boat around first. More knee pull, leave the head in until last. This cannot be exaggerated too much, and there is no point in going to the next lesson until this one is mastered.

When all have been in the canoe, have them kneel along the edge of the pool with their paddles for paddle brace practice. They should be able to put their faces in the water and recover with the paddle. Many will fall in.

Now show them how the whole stroke feels. You kneel in front, have them kneel behind. You go through the stroke using your muscle memory, they mimic you. Watch them and correct errors. Someone will say this isn't what you did when you rolled. They are confused by the relative motion. They should do as you say and not try to think. Drill them thoroughly on this motion while they are on land and easily corrected.

This is enough for the first lesson. The determined students will think through the roll over and over before the next class. The others will progress slowly.

On the second session, review the land drill. In the canoe, review the wrist-hip roll. If they do it well, give them the paddle. The left hand is in the normal position on top of the paddle. The right hand moves up 6 to 12 inches from the throat to ease the reach, and the right wrist is arched to take the strain.

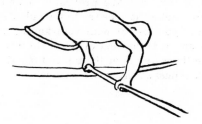

At first, hold their blade tip just below the surface so the paddle is perpendicular to the canoe. Have them put their head in the water, then bring the canoe over with their hips, turn the canoe back, and finally bring their head up again. Emphasize bringing the knee and canoe up more forcibly, leaving the head in until last. You will probably have to put a hand under their armpit and lift them back from the underworld. When this is mastered, they are ready to try the complete roll - with someone standing by to give a helping push on the canoe at the critical moment.

The complete roll goes like this. You are paddling on the right and it will be a right roll. Tip over either way. Put your paddle along the left side of the canoe, blade forward, top by your hip. Shift your right hand up from the throat and arch that wrist. Sweep the paddle blade in an arc, aft sculling along the surface of the water. Start pulling on your right knee. Your arms come up over your head as the paddle comes perpendicular to the canoe. This is the positioning stroke, and you are now ready for the power drive. It is an awkward position with little power at first, but it is important that the blade start near the surface or it will go too deep and you will fail. Now the paddle is flipped over, rotated forward, so the other side of the blade is down. Now drive the paddle, arms, head, and torso down to the right, pulling up sharply with the right knee. Sweep, flip, drive! After the canoe is around, you get your body up just as you did on the edge of the pool. Push down with the right hand, pull up with the left.

The pictures of this roll are presented in an unorthodox way – as it seems to the roller, not as it appears to the onlooker. The canoe is the frame of reference; you feel it with your knees, and in all pictures it is flat and right side up. It is the rest of the world that you are turning over. In the first picture the water is at the top and the air at the bottom. In the last picture you have pushed the water back where it belongs – underneath you.

Sweep the paddle blade aft in an arc at or near the surface. Start pulling your right knee up.

The end of the positioning stroke finds the paddle perpendicular to the canoe. The canoe has only started to turn relative to the water surface.

Quickly the paddle is flipped over bringing the wrist high, ready for the power drive.

92

Now drive your torso, head, arms, and paddle down to the right and pull up sharply and powerfully with your right knee.

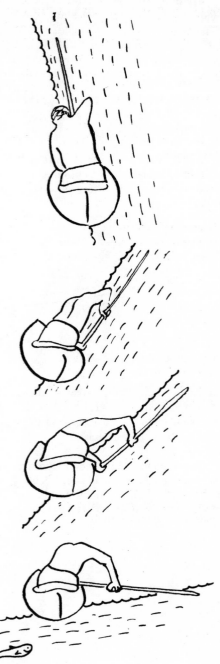

As you drive, you get the right elbow up so you are on top of the paddle. Knees and hips bring the canoe around while the head is still in the water.

The canoe now has a righting moment and helps you. If the paddle sinks too deep, you will not make it.

At the very end the body is brought aboard by prying up, up with the left hand, down with the right.

Common reasons for failure are: You tried to think and became confused, your paddle did not start near the surface on the power drive or was not perpendicular to the canoe, the flip was too slow and lost depth, or the paddle blade was not flat. However, the most common reason is not enough hip action and knee pull. When the head comes up first, there has not been enough hip action and the head will sink back in. If you will wear a face mask, it will help you discover your faults. Of course, you must learn to do it with your eyes closed. Above all, compare your motions in dry air runs, with those of a successful roller. So it is, that you will develop the correct muscle memory.

It will take a hundred rolls in still water and some deliberate upsets in rapids before your Eskimo roll becomes a reliable white water skill. In the meantime, working on your roll will greatly improve your paddle brace.

The slalom canoe permits the challenge of more difficult rapids, and opens spectacular rivers of great beauty to the canoeist. It makes possible a wholly new facet of playing the river, a dashing approach to canoeing in which the key is attack.

These canoes will become very popular, but they will supplement and not supplant the open canoe. The open canoe has its advantages for long northwoods voyages even for the experts. The mass of paddlers will continue to use the open canoe for many years to come.

CHAPTER 11

ENJOYING RIVER CANOEING

This little book has tried to open a door to you; a door to a world of beauty, a life of rich experiences, and a companionship with wonderful people. As you enter, we ask one thing of you. This world cannot continue to exist unless all who enter will adhere to the ethics of outdoors people and support the canoeing sport in proportion to their pleasure in it.

We leave our camp sites cleaner than we found them. Often we pick up after others. We do not want it thought that any canoeist would leave litter, and the next canoeist to come by will be happier for our effort. There is a growing feeling that camp sites should be natural without trenching of tents and building of tables. Many of us are happiest with an "unimproved" camp site and after we have enjoyed it we slip away leaving it so the next party is sure they are the first men to have set eyes on this beautiful spot.

The rivers of America belong to the people, a privilege not enjoyed in all countries. However, the laws of our states vary as to whether the bottom is private property and the rights of portage have not been settled in courts of law. Certainly the shores with their tent sites and lunch spots are private. There is a strong sense of private property and many landowners do not realize the public may coast down the streams. May we ask that you do not try to argue your rights, but instead make friends with the landowners. Get permissions as needed, and help build a reputation that canoeists are unlike other hordes from the city so that canoeists are welcome wherever water flows.

Fishermen and all whom you meet must be treated with consideration. They have gone to a remote spot for a purpose and you must not barge past and spoil their day. Slip silently past on the opposite shore so they cannot possibly think you scared the fish.

For river running, you will need a group to run with for safety, learning, and car shuttle arrangements. If there is a local club, join. Otherwise, you will be forming a group around you. It need not be a formal club but you must see that the standards of safety and canoeing skills are high, and that you welcome others to the sport as you have been welcomed.

You must make realistic appraisals of your canoeing ability. As a graduate of Red Ridge College, or any like course, you are not yet a skilled river canoeist. You have had the way pointed out and it is now up to you to develop your potential. You must assimilate what you have just learned by applying it; only experience can make the new knowledge a part of you. The most useful yardstick of your ability is the river rating system.

The international system of river rating was devised to help you pick the trips you can handle safely. It was carefully thought through, considering the skill required and the danger incurred if the skill proved inadequate. Canoeists paddling in other countries compare their judgment of ratings to try to make the system uniform the world over. The agreed-upon descriptions are given in the appendix. Of course, ice cold water will make any river more dangerous than its rating, and so will abnormal flood water. You will rate your ability by the rivers you have run. However, just having run a Grade III river does not qualify you for Grade IV. Was it really Grade III the day you ran it? Did you sneak through on luck, or did you master the river? You do not go on to Grade IV until you are already a Grade IV paddler from playing the rapids in Grade III rivers.

Where will you go in your canoe? Once we had to use our own imagination. We counted contour lines on maps, studied stream flow records, and tried rivers where the natives were sure no canoe could go. Today there are many guide books and you will find a partial list in the appendix. They were compiled by enthusiasts like you with much personal labor and expense. We are indebted to them. The job is, however, not finished. Outstanding rivers worthy of expeditions from afar need strip maps, and full information on the natural wonders and the historic sites. Every local stream with a day of paddling that lies near a town where there may someday be a scout troop, deserves to be included in a guide that is cheaply sold and widely distributed in the area. There is opportunity for you to carry on the work so well begun.

You have gained much from the national canoeing organizations and should give them your support. Time was when the canoeist was an independent soul who fled into the wilderness where no one would disturb him.

Tomorrow that wilderness will be taken away if you do not forego your isolationism and cooperate with other canoeists to preserve it. Help others to share your sport and your wilderness. It will be saved only if enough people learn how to use it and to appreciate it. Join one of the national organizations, either the ancient and honorable American Canoe Association or the evangelistic American Whitewater Affiliation. Give them a hand with their projects.

The canoeist of tomorrow must even participate in government and civic affairs. He must write letters to support the cause of conservation nationally, he must watch state legislation lest it impose harmful regulations on canoeing, and he must battle for clean streams locally. Our governments become more and more interested in recreation as a cure for various social ills. Will the knowledgeable sportsmen help in the planning? Of what good are the open spaces being set aside if people do not know how to use them properly? It is surely a time when the youth organizations could use your help.

To some people canoe slalom is anathema. How can a physical and artificial competition have meaning when the true values are nature and wilderness? Yet, in just a few years, slalom has revolutionized canoeing and in doing so contributed much to wilderness canoeing. It has improved techniques so that wilderness rapids are safer today. It has publicized and popularized canoeing to gain more support for wild river bills. It has attracted capable youngsters into canoeing. When their competitive drive wanes, they will run wilderness white water and throw their talent into the conservation battles. Do frequent slaloms, talk with all the canoeists, and have a fling at it yourself.

The door is open. You may see the fun and the beauty, the obligations and the opportunities. Do enter.

APPENDIX

GUIDEBOOKS

Walter Burmeister, "Appalachian Water," 2 vols., 1962
    (Privately printed by The Canoe Cruisers Association
    of Washington, D. C., and now unavailable.)
A. M. C., "The A. M. C. New England Canoeing Guide," 1965
    $5.00, The Appalachian Mountain Club, 5 Joy Street,
    Boston, Mass. 02108
Lawrence I. Grinnell, "Canoeable Waterways of New York State
    and Vicinity" - 1956, Pageant Press, New York
James and Margaret Cawley, "Exploring the Little Rivers of New Jersey,"
    Princeton University Press, Princeton, N. J.
Randy Carter, "Canoeing White Water in Northern Virginia and North-
    eastern West Virginia, also The Great Smoky Mountain Area,"
    4th ed. 1963, $3.50, Louis Matacia, 3430 Lee Highway,
    Fairfax, Va. 22030
Oz Hawksley, "Missouri Ozark Waterways," 1965, $1.00, Missouri
    Conservation Commission, Jefferson City, Mo. 65101
Andres Peekna, "Guide to White Water in the Wisconsin Area,"
    1967, $1.25, Outing Director, The Wisconsin Union, Univ.
    of Wisconsin, 800 Langdon Street, Madison, Wis. 53706.

STATE PAMPLETS

"Maine Canoeing," Maine Devel. Comm., Augusta, Me. 04330
"About Stream Canoeing in New Hampshire," State Planning and
    Devel. Comm., Concord, N. H. 03301
"Adirondack Canoe Routes," Circular 7, Conservation Dept., Albany,
    New York 12224
"Lake George," Circular 6, State Conservation Dept., Albany, N. Y. 12224
"Canoeing in Tennessee," Dept. of Conservation, Nashville, Tenn. 37219
"Canoe Trails of Michigan," Michigan Tourist Council, Lansing, Mich. 48924
"Wisconsin Water Trails," Wisconsin Conservation Dept., Madison, Wis. 53702

"Canoe Trips," (Quetico-Superior Park), Canoe Country Outfitters,
    Ely, Minn. 55731
"Canoeing in Canada," Canadian Government Travel Bureau,
    Ottawa, Canada
"Canoe Routes to Hudson Bay," Dept. of the Interior, Ottawa, Canada

INSTRUCTION BOOKS - FLAT WATER

"Canoeing," American National Red Cross, 1956, 445 pages
"Basic Canoeing," American National Red Cross, 1963, 63 pages
"Canoeing," Merit Badge Series, Boy Scouts of America, 1939

INSTRUCTION BOOKS - WHITE WATER

John T. Urban, "A White Water Handbook for Canoe and Kayak,"
    Appalachian Mountain Club, 5 Joy Street, Boston, Mass. 02108,
    1965, $1.50
Peter D. Whitney, "White Water Sport," 1960, $4.50, Ronald Press,
    New York
Jay Evans, "Fundamentals of Kayaking," 1964, Ledyard Canoe Club,
    Dartmouth College, Hanover, N. H. 03755
George G. Siposs, "From Start To Finish," 1964, A manual for whitewater
    competitors, "Haystackers," c/o Paul Kipers, 1304 Truitt St.,
    Glendale, Calif. 91201

NATIONAL CANOEING ORGANIZATIONS

American Whitewater Affiliation, c/o Harold Kiehm, 2019 Addison Street,
    Chicago, Illinois 60618. Dues of $3.50 will bring you "American
    Whitewater" quarterly.
American Canoe Association, c/o Ted Alteneder, Jr., 1217 Spring Garden
    Street, Philadelphia, Pa. 19123. Dues of $4.00 plus initiation fee
    will bring you the quarterly magazine, "The American Canoeist."
United States Canoe Association, c/o Charles Moore, 6338 Hoover Road,
    Indianapolis, Indiana 46260. Dues of $4.00 bring you the newsletter
    of this dynamic young organization.

APPENDIX 2

INTERNATIONAL SCALE FOR GRADING THE DIFFICULTY OF RIVER CRUISING ROUTES

Rating	River or Individual Rapids Characteristics	Approx. Minimum Experience Req'd.
Smooth Water		
A	Pools, Lakes, Rivers with velocity under 2 miles per hour.	Beginner
B	Rivers, velocity 2-4 mph	Beginner with River Instruction
C	Rivers, velocity above 1 mph (max. back-paddling speed) may have some sharp bends and/or obstructions.	Instructed and Practiced Beginner
White Water		
I	Easy—Sand-banks, bends without difficulty, occasional small rapids with waves regular and low. Correct course easy to find but care is needed with minor obstacles like pebble banks, fallen trees, etc., especially on narrow rivers. River speed less than hard back paddling speed.	Practiced Beginner
II	Medium—Fairly frequent but unobstructed rapids, usually with regular waves easy eddies and easy bends. Course generally easy to recognize. River speeds occasionally exceeding hard back paddling speed.	Intermediate
III	Difficult—Maneuvering in rapids necessary. Small falls, large regular waves covering boat, numerous rapids. Main current may swing under bushes, branches or overhangs. Course not always easily recognizable. Current speed usually less than fast forward paddling speed.	Experienced
IV	Very Difficult—Long extended stretches of rapids, high irregular waves with boulders directly in current. Difficult broken water, eddies, and abrupt bends. Course often difficult to recognize and inspection from the bank frequently necessary. Swift current. Rough water experience indispensable.	Highly Skilled (several years experience with organized group)
V	Exceedingly Difficult—Long rocky rapids with difficult and completely irregular broken water which must be run head on. Very fast eddies, abrupt bends and vigorous cross currents. Difficult landings increase hazard. Frequent inspections neecssary. *Extensive* experience neecssary.	Team of Experts
VI	Limit of Navigability—All previously-mentioned difficulties increased to the limit. Only negotiable at favorable water levels. *Cannot be attempted without risk of life.*	Team of Experts (taking every precaution)

American WHITE WATER

APPENDIX 3

RULES FOR CANOE SLALOM

A canoe slalom is a race through an obstacle course set in a river rapids. The gates are cleared in order, red pole to left, green to right, and penalties are added to running time if any gates are touched or missed. Full rules of the International Canoe Federation can be obtained from the National Slalom Chairman of the American Canoe Association.

A typical course has fifteen or more gates in a Grade III rapid. Each gate consists of two 5-foot poles, 1-1/2 inches in diameter, hanging 4 feet apart. The left pole has 5 red and 5 white stripes, the right pole has 5 green and 5 white stripes. A "free" gate has 5 black and 5 white stripes on both poles. In all cases the stripe closest to the water is white. Each gate is numbered and in addition the reverse gates carry the letter "R" and the team gate is marked "T". Gates are usually suspended from wires that span the river.

The winner is the competitor with the lowest score, the score being the sum of running time in seconds plus penalties incurred. Each competitor is allowed two runs in each class entered; his better run is counted. There usually are classes for C-2 men, C-2 mixed, C-1 men, K-1 men, and K-1 women.

Clearing of Gates

Gates must be cleared in numbered sequence and in respect to their directional colors. A gate is cleared when the bow (stern for reverse gates) and the body or bodies have crossed the LBP, the imaginary Line Between Poles. A free gate may be cleared forward or backward from either side.

Penalties are assessed for each gate:

Each pole touched - add 10 seconds

The touch may be by paddle, body, or canoe. Several touches on the same pole incur only a single penalty. Touching both poles incurs 20 seconds. These touching penalties, however, are not added on top of the heavier penalties for missing gates.

Gate touched and missed - add 50 seconds
    If the gate is touched by canoe or body, but the bow and bodies do not cross the LBP, then a 50-second penalty is incurred. A common case is the "outside touch" where the canoe hits the outside of the pole in passing. Going through a red and green gate from the wrong side or with bow and stern wrongly oriented also incurs a 50-second penalty.

    A penalty once incurred cannot be erased by further attempts. Only the first engagement of a gate is counted. It starts when any part of the canoe crosses the LBP or with any touch of either pole.

Gate missed entirely - add 100 seconds
    A gate is considered missed if it has not been cleared before the gate of next higher number is engaged. A gate is also ruled as missed if a touch by paddle is not immediately followed by crossing the LBP or touching with canoe or body.

    The possible penalties for one gate are therefore 0, 10, 20, 50 or 100 seconds.

    When a gate is cleared and the stern has also crossed the LBP no further penalties can be incurred by later touches of that gate. The gate following the one being attempted is valid and dangerous, but subsequent gates do not yet exist. (Touching Gate 5 while trying for Gate 3 incurs no penalty.)

    A capsize not followed by an Eskimo roll disqualfies the competitor, as does leaving his canoe.

Team Race
    There are three canoes on each team and time is taken from the first canoe across the start to the last across the finish. Penalties on all three canoes are added so careful precision pays off in this event. There is an added 50-second penalty if the three canoes do not pass through the designated team gate within 15 seconds.

THE ENGLISH GATE TEST

This test is done through a single slalom gate set in still water and is an excellent training idea. It can be set in a swimming pool. It has been used as a qualification test, as a competition, and as a public demonstration. For training, it gives a measure of improvement as the paddler gains skill. It also allows comparison between canoes or techniques.

The test consists of four figures done through a slalom gate against a stop watch. Memorizing them is facilitated by noting that the last two figures are the first two done backward, and that the rolls are done inward after passing the pole on the outside. No pole touchings are permitted!

Start

1. Forward pivots.

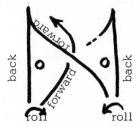

2. Back on outside, forward diagonals.

3. Back pivots.

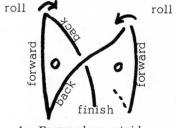

4. Forward on outside, back diagonals.

Cruising canoes must, of course, pass up the Eskimo rolls. A record for the single seat kayak is 72 seconds.

APPENDIX 6